RACING LEXICON

RACING
LEXICON

LEIGH & WOODHOUSE

faber and faber

First published in 2005
by Faber and Faber Limited
3 Queen Square, London, WC1N 3AU

Photoset by RefineCatch Limited, Bungay, Suffolk
Printed in England by Mackays of Chatham, plc

A CIP record for this book
is available from the British Library

ISBN 0-571-22989-1

Acknowledgements

Leigh and Woodhouse would like to thank Woodhouse's father Frank
for his invaluable comments on the text, and Jonathan Pritchard for
his many helpful suggestions.

Thanks also to: Carabelli Café, Melanie Cole, Jack de Flamingh,
Gary Eaborn, Claire Guyon, Alan Juckes, Michael Leigh, Ita
Maccarthy, National Horseracing Museum (Newmarket), Kiaran
'Yeti' Saunders and friends, Jonty Woodhouse.

2 4 6 8 10 9 7 5 3 1

Preface

'Everyone says I can't read or write, which is garbage. I can get through the *Sporting Life* in about ten minutes.' Jimmy White's assertion goes some way to proving that a grounding in the three Rs is essential for any serious fan of racing. And, in addition to speed-reading and filling out his own betting slips, the snooker player's real strength lies in his whirlwind grasp of the mathematical permutations. According to his former manager, Barry Hearn, 'Jimmy would work out a ***Yankee*** in ten seconds, but couldn't name the capital of France.' It is perhaps a pity that someone who normally studies all the angles has missed out on the pleasure of reading the 'Prognostications of Omar Sharif', which appear in a Sunday newspaper supplement when a big betting heat takes place at Longchamp or Auteuil. Such an avid punter would, however, immediately identify with the efforts of French racegoers to catch up on essential reading. If it is debatable whether racing is the sport that generates the most talk, it must be indisputable that it is the sport that generates the most paper. Even though the process of betting requires slightly less arithmetical prowess in a city which may have lent its name to

pari-mutuel wagering, you can still *rip up your slips*
after the last race and throw them away with your
Paris Turf and your dreams of being up for the day.

The fact that much of their research material ends
up on the floors of the racecourse enclosures after
the *lucky last* should not detract from the fact that
the written word is of fundamental importance to all
racing people, whichever enclosure they choose to
stand in. It is not an accident that racing remains the
only sport in Britain, and indeed the only pursuit
other than finance, that has a national daily paper
devoted to it. Anybody who is at the races other than
for purely social reasons will have something printed
in their hand for most of the afternoon, starting with
the *Racing Post* itself, which by 1998 had done for the
Sporting Life rather in the way Stephen Hendry had
done for Jimmy White. Other items to be devoured by
racegoers even more hungrily than smoked salmon
and hog roasts may include: the racecard produced
by the course, the analysis from a preferred tabloid
they have cut or ripped out, a Timeform or other
specialised rating guide, or some tip-sheet they were
foolish enough to buy outside the door.

The same need for printed material is evident
wherever racing takes place, even in those countries
where there is no newspaper of daily record. Once,
when on our way to a race meeting in Vancouver,
we were set down by our taxi at the wrong venue, as
became immediately apparent. Not only were the
people in the entrance queue too uniformly smart
(even at Royal Ascot there are areas where you can
escape the dress code) but none of them was holding
any reading matter. The punters in question turned
out to be Jehovah's Witnesses attending a convention, whereas the racetrack was situated at the
other end of Hastings Park. True to form, once we
had jogged across to the course to preserve some
preparation time before the opening race, we quickly

came across a bar where horseplayers of varying social backgrounds and varying degrees of bookishness were united in poring over a vast quantity of newsprint. But for a simulcast from Belmont blaring over the TV screens and the Molson on tap, the atmosphere would have been something akin to a prayer meeting.

Robert Runcie, an Archbishop of Canterbury who enjoyed attending the odd race meeting, once observed: 'All religions need a sacred text and Timeform is racing's Bible.' For connections of an animal demonised by that publication as a *squiggle horse* it can be hard to look past such a seminal work. Yet it may be truer to say that racing has a number of sacred texts, all known more profanely as 'books', which govern the operations of the sport and generate a specialised lexicon, over and above the technical language concerned with equine conformation and husbandry.

Certainly, the sport's Book of Life is the *General Stud Book*, established by James Weatherby in 1791 to provide a reliable record of every thoroughbred horse, tracing their ancestry back to three Arab foundation sires imported into England. A racehorse must, even to this day, appear 'in the book' or its overseas equivalents in order to be eligible to run at most of the world's licensed courses. Breeding is a lifelong hobby for the many British and Irish enthusiasts who produce home-breds, and a multi-million-pound industry for the larger commercial operations. Coolmore and Godolphin both look at the bottom line in terms of hard cash as well as the dam's pedigree. The economics of breeding sometimes affect the way races themselves are described: mares can be running for *black type* as much as prize money and, if a colt wins in devastating style, some journalists will be thinking about what cover fee he will command, as he is likely to be retired from racing sooner rather than later. Breeding also works its way into everyday racing language because it is undeniably true that pedigree matters. The way ability and temperament are passed on from generation to generation is something that fascinates and exasperates those who study the family trees printed in sales catalogues and racecards. Sons and daughters of **Strong Gale** will have a strong tendency to behave like and, more importantly, run like their sire.

Trainers trying to place horses with an inherited inability to stay a certain distance or act on certain ground will tell their owners they will 'have a look in the book' for a suitable race, by which they mean the **programme book**, or *Racing Calendar*, which lists the conditions of all races at upcoming meetings. A crucial part of a trainer's skill, perhaps even more important than getting a horse fit, is to find him the easiest winning opportunities. In Britain and Ireland, the tradition in the lower echelons of the sport is for there to be more handicaps than claimers, and so the game of cat-and-mouse between trainer and handicapper, as the one tries to delay the moment that his horse's ability is **exposed** to the other, engenders a colourful set of metaphors which can suggest military precision, criminal stealth or, for the best **coups** of all, a combination of the two. Meanwhile, in the higher grades, since the mid 1960s the *Pattern Book* has concentrated the minds of owners and trainers on the major international races of the season and focused the dreams of those who may turn out to be also-rans. Every **renewal** of these great contests reminds us of the stuff of legend that hovers about the racing calendar – the horses whose names are inscribed in the roll of honour and who have achieved the 'classic' designation themselves. The memory of these **equine** legends will always be enough to encourage tilting ambitions each season.

Of all the books in racing, that made up by professional layers is the most touted and the least bookish.

Before computer technology, these ledgers were huge,
unwieldy tomes in which every bet was recorded in
longhand. When a bookie's mate writing down each
wager referred to an 'uneven book', he was not complaining about having nowhere to lean on but warning his boss that liabilities were dangerously high
on one horse and that their book was out of line with
the rest of the market. Independent bookmaking is
rightly a source of grievance for most other parties
in the industry because less profit is reinvested into
racing; England, Ireland and Australia are unusual
in that betting on horses is not entirely monopolised
by the state. But however much they take out of
the game, bookies add a priceless amount of excitement to the sport and colour to the lexicon. Roving
reporter Alan Partridge may have thought that the
men in white gloves he saw standing on soapboxes at
Sandown Park were catering for the deaf, but *tic-tac*
is just the most obvious form of special language used
when bets are feverishly being struck and laid off.
The argot also includes rhyming slang – 'making
a docker's hook' is a self-referential example – and
backslang such as *exes*. The betting ring for a big race,
with its frantic inflows and outflows, is a microcosm
of a liquid capital market. Observing or participating
is an undeniably exciting experience, and a colloquial
language is in place to reflect the activity: punters get
stuck into *steamers* and sometimes get burned as a
result, while the fact that bookies usually fill their
satchels makes it all the more satisfying when we
make them run for cover. It is perhaps telling that in
America, a country where the *pari-mutuel* system
reigns, the most common colloquialism for favourite
is 'the chalk', a term which pines for the age when
bookies chalked up the prices on their *boards*.

Most market leaders are entitled to go close 'on
the book', meaning the *form book*, something which
physically exists in racing and which dominates the

thinking of serious form students. With the arrival
of the internet and devoted racing channels on satel-
lite, the informed punter has an array of tools to
interpret the value of the bare form, and the role of
the race-reader may have become less important.
However, for anybody who has not actually seen the
race in question, the on-course reporter who writes
potted remarks on every horse's performance provides a valuable source of information and terminology. There is a set, abbreviated form of language used
for these comments-in-running that is functional and
undeceived. Connections will convince themselves
that their horse was unlucky to lose his position at
halfway, only to run on very encouragingly in the
closing stages – until they read in the *Racing Post* the
next morning: 'Always behind'; or, if they are lucky:
'Held up in midfield, lost place 5f out, no danger
after.' The prose of race-reading can be stark and
often unforgiving, but it is a form of telegraphese
reminiscent of Mr Jingle's manner in *The Pickwick
Papers*. Sometimes there is an equally graphic effect
as the writer tries to compress the exciting events of
the race into clipped reportage. Here is an example
from a Conditions Stakes at Wolverhampton: 'Held
up, headway over 4f out, led well over 1f out, ridden
and hung right inside final furlong, soon jinked badly
left and nearly unseated rider, ran on'. The 'ran on' is
a typically nice understatement here.

If race-readers always seek vocabulary which provides the greatest narrative economy, professionals
within the game will sometimes be in search of a discourse which is economical with the truth. Perhaps
because they can never hear it straight from their
horse's mouth, **connections** are forever talking to
each other, in hope before a race and – much more
often than not – disappointment afterwards. These
discussions will centre on how to place the beast
to best advantage in the future ('He'll want better

ground,' 'He'll appreciate a longer trip'), often as a way of avoiding any realistic assessment of the animal's ability. One of the most crucial of all these different conversations is the report a jockey gives to connections immediately after a race. Owners, and sometimes even trainers, will hang on his every word in rapt anticipation of the key to the horse being found. A jockey's response is of course governed by self-interest: he will usually want to keep the ride, even if the horse will never win, in order to retain ties with the trainer, and even if he has found the trainer's own pre-race instructions about the horse being *keen* to be rather understated. But, as well as softening his words like any bringer of bad tidings, the jockey can also seem on many occasions to be swept up in his sport's habitual determination to look on the bright side. Therefore his thoughts will be self-translated into a different form of words: 'He's an idle sod who *dogs it* at the first opportunity and *keeps something for himself*' comes out as 'Perhaps he needs blinkers just to sharpen him up a bit'. Or: 'He really is the slowest horse I've sat on this year and we'd still not have finished if I hadn't pulled him up' is reconfigured for the benefit of connections thus: 'He'll appreciate *every inch* of three miles on soft ground at Towcester or Chepstow.'

Part of a jockey's weighing-room education is therefore a kind of creative writing course enabling him to tell connections what they want to hear. It is easy to be cynical about these exercises in communal self-delusion, which are then continued by the trainer back in the owners' and trainers' bar. Yet they can rather be viewed as an endearing example of the way racing people keep themselves going even when their horses are not having *going days*. This should be particularly true when you consider the fact that the majority of jockeys and trainers do not have much cause to work out their *percentage* and continue to do their jobs for

love as much as money. There is indeed a tension for
racing professionals, which finds expression in both
their behaviour and their language, between hard-
headed economics and an enthusiasm for the sport
and the animals which goes beyond the betting and
the business. On the one hand, there is a cynical and
world-weary edge to much of the trade's terminology,
exemplified by the countless euphemisms available
for circumstances where a horse receives overenthusi-
astic *assistance*, gets injured or killed, or is simply
terribly – and expensively – slow. On the other, there
is a great energy in many racing terms, such as the
extremely colourful metaphors designed to convey the
excitement of races and the thrill of the gallop, while
a high register is maintained to express admiration
for the *doughty* steeds who run for our pleasure and
benefit. However, just as the prospect of winning her
bet at the races prompted Eliza Doolittle to forget (or
perhaps recall) herself and her language, so the earthy
presence of gambling, with which the sport of kings
has always had a Faustian pact, will often check any
sentimental, romantic tendency.

Hugh McIlvanney once observed that 'people who
think racing is not about gambling probably think
that dancing is not about sex'; Paul Eddington, whose
father had a serious gambling problem, compared
placing a bet to the sexual act: 'A lengthy period of
preparation and anticipation, followed by a quick
burst of excitement, followed by an equally lengthy
period of regret.' While it may be risky to develop
these ideas, it is generally true that in the excitement
phase, as we shout the runners *home*, what we scream
will tend to be monosyllabic ('Come on A.P.!').
Whereas in the lengthy periods before and after, most
punters will not only light a cigarette but talk the hind
legs off a donkey.

Premium rate tipping lines, however risible their
advertisements – 'THREE MASSIVE WINNERS

THIS WEEK ALREADY! [SPs 1/2, 4/6, 30/100; 6 other runners advised]' – exploit the punter's basic need to hear as much information as possible before placing a bet. And indeed, through racing history, a premium has always been placed on any such information which is thought to be privileged, the proverbial *whisper*. There are lots of ways of saying you have heard that a reliable contact has been told that a certain horse is quietly fancied, so quietly that the 20/1 generally available in the morning seems to have contracted to 5/2 by the time you get to the ring. When the *jolly* duly loses, punters have a basic need to let off steam and explain why everything they said before the race was misconceived. The Betfair chatroom now records in the form of furiously typed emails the things gamblers have always said to each other when the nailed on favourite comes unstuck: 'I could have given it a better ride with one finger'; 'The trainer of the winner's a criminal'; 'The whole game is b–nt' (a word so injurious to racing's reputation that it is considered to be a blockable expletive by the exchange's website). You will also meet on any racecourse self-styled big players who will regale you with the gigantic *touches* they have already pulled off or are planning. It is always curious that losses never seem to appear in their verbal betting ledger, especially now that they can call themselves traders on the exchanges rather than punters in an office, but the braggadocio of these characters adds another rich seam to racing's lexicon.

There was a time when not only the language of such characters but any allusion to their very existence was silenced in the commentaries of the BBC, whose Governors prohibited any talk of starting prices, lest viewers resorted *en masse* to off-course gambling. In those days, therefore, racing commentary was devoted to describing an apparently pure sporting spectacle unsullied by odds and prices. Yet if racing commentary

these days is not ashamed to be a vehicle for telling us
what is happening to our stake, it requires skill which
deserves also to impress those without money riding
on the race. The standard of racecourse commentary in
Britain and Ireland remains, even after the retirement
of Sir Peter O'Sullevan, the Voice of Racing, incons-
picuously high, and the occasional exception proves
the difficulty of the assignment. A racing commentator
calls the horses – that is, he calls them by their names.
This is a convention, or perhaps an unwritten rule,
which does not extend to greyhound racing, where
numbers prevail during the race. The barrage of dis-
parate names unleashed in a *cavalry charge* will
sometimes create a sort of dizzying surreal poetry.
Racing talk and commentary can activate otherwise
improbable statements like 'Toulouse-Lautrec is relish-
ing this slog in the mud.' The flow of racing commentary often then depends on the suppression of
references or sources behind these names – commentators need not only to know the names, but to ignore
their real meanings. Yet names are sometimes also a
resource as well a distraction for the commentator,
and they can spawn their own idioms. Thus, as we
heard, 'Sir Cumference shaping well after a year's
absence.'

But calling the horses, as the verb implies, involves
not only naming, but proclaiming or indeed simply
shouting. Race commentary is a performance, a sort
of litany. The crescendo in a racing commentor's
voice is integral to any description of a race. Peter
O'Sullevan, in particular, was a master of monotone
in the early stages of a race, particularly if it was
tactical. The pace of a horse tends to generate a com-
mensurate speed in the voice of the commentator.
Many commentators duly move up a semitone or two
to signify a change in pace. They will tend to shout as
the winner comes home, mirroring in the strain of
their voices the likelihood that the horse is at full pelt,

before, as the horse pulls up, bringing the voice down accordingly with a rallentando. The metre and music of these incantations will not compensate punters after another loss, but their familiar rhythms may go some way to reconciling us to the inevitable.

Live commentary is not only essential to televised racing (such that if you are watching a long-distance chase from Naas which is interrupted by a *split-screen* for the 2.48 from Catford, the loss of sound will seriously impair the aesthetic enjoyment) but integral to the experience of racing at the course itself. Few if any sports provide commentary in running at the venue. It follows that commentators can create the very experience they are describing. When a historic race is recalled in the mind's eye, it will be accompanied by the exact words in which it was described at the time: 'It's *hats* off and a tremendous reception – you've never heard one like it at Liverpool!'

Ultimately, though, all the exuberance and the evocative powers of race commentary throw into relief the simple truth that the horses which are its subject cannot speak. Yet they too have things to tell us. It was not a *talking horse* but a member of one of Ireland's great racing dynasties, Tom Taafe, who said: 'In the racing game, the horse tells you when to go.' It is to him, or rather to his Cheltenham Gold Cup winner Kicking King, that we give the last word. Weeks before the race, the horse had been laid low by an infection, and Taafe had reluctantly decided to pull him out of the contest: 'Within seventy-two hours, Kicking King was so mad fresh in his field he almost jumped over his gate. It was his way of telling me to bring him to Cheltenham. He was so well he said to come here.' Traders who heard the initial health bulletin and tried to *buy money* by laying the horse on the exchanges may have a less romantic take on this insider information straight from the horse's mouth. It is also easy to become over-sentimental about the telepathic understanding which can seem to develop between man and *beast*, for trainers can become as easily frustrated by the fact that horses cannot say what might be amiss with them. But it is the horses who tell us in some indefinable way that they would be champions. While the racing lexicon is spoken and written by a host of human characters – breeders, owners, stewards, trainers, stable lads and lasses, jockeys, journalists, commentators, bookies, punters – the history of racing is scripted in the long run by the horses themselves.

A

Abba: In their ongoing attempts to persuade the general public that a day at the races is not just about betting on horses, British racecourses not only try to make the very best of the *facilities* they have to offer but also organise entertainment during and after summer meetings. If names like Abba Kadabra, Bjorn Again and Super Troopers appear in the racecard, these will not be horses but *Abba* tribute bands lined up for the post-race show. Punters find a special sense of bittersweetness in the line: 'I feel like I win when I lose.'

Ability: 'More *temperament* than *ability*': this is the withering shorthand sometimes seen in racecards to dismiss the chances of a particular horse. It could also summarise the general balance of probabilities for a breed where the price of athleticism is to be highly strung or, to use a more dignified term, *high-mettled*. Certainly, the *ability* of a racehorse is usually remarked upon when it is compromised by fragility of legs or mind, or when it is ebbing away. So if a trainer protests that one of his horses '*retains plenty* of *ability*', it may be safe to assume that the animal does not retain much *zest*.

About: 'The sponsor is now offering 12/1 *about* the winner for the Tote Gold Trophy.' It is a strange little habit of betting parlance that this preposition seems to be used more when you are talking of *ante-post* odds than starting prices. The following is a standard formulation after the event: 'Marble Arch was *sent off* the 9/2 favourite in the Newbury *feature*.'

Accept the situation: What a jockey does when he *stops riding*, or even pulls a horse up, because he is resigned to not *making the frame*: 'Aveiro never got into *top gear* and in the end Dean Williams *accepted the situation*.' Punters who have backed the horse in question are not always quite so sanguine.

Acey-deucy: 'There have been many variations on the current fashionable European method of riding: for instance *acey-deucy* – one stirrup longer than the other – used by Yanks to assist in negotiating corners.' This quotation is from an Australian daily newspaper, but it defines the style patented by Eddie Arcaro, where the inside **iron** (almost invariably the left on American tracks with tight left *turns*) is worn *longer*, allegedly to promote better balance and control. The derivation may be from cards (where the phrase can mean 'one-two') or more likely backgammon (whose variant game *acey-deucy* is also known as 'high-low'). *Acey-deucy* has also come to mean 'bisexual' in American slang, but the racing usage probably pre-dates any suggestion that the jockey could ride two ways.

Across: The operative word when the *draw* is a *factor* and a jockey with a high-numbered *berth* tries to get his horse out and *over* quickly into a good position further on the inside, preferably the rails: 'Stan tried to get her *across* to the *fence* but there was little chance from the *outside alley*.' See also **boards**

and **card** for the preposition's appearance in betting contexts.

Action: Horses are said to have an *action* when they **bowl along**, although you tend to hear about it most when they have *lost* it. But some race summarisers become technical enough to refer viewers to the *round* or *knee-high action* of the mud-lover compared to the more *choppy* or *daisy-cutting action* of a horse who likes it *on top*. The former type may therefore not *act* on **sharp** courses or firm ground.

Admirable: 'The thoroughly *admirable* Lygeton Lad goes for yet another *all-weather* win'; 'The *admirable* Vinnie Roe was *better than ever* at the age of six, winning the Irish St Leger for a remarkable fourth time.' The kind of adjective reserved for **old** *soldiers* who seem to *stand* their *racing* particularly well.

Aeroplane: The power of a car's engine is still measured in *horsepower* (even after the demise of the Citroen *2 chevaux*) and, as many subsequent entries will testify, racing frequently returns the favour. Racehorses can, however, be compared to other forms of transportation: 'In some ways I'm sorry to be retiring as David's got a stable full of *aeroplanes* this year.'

Agent: In his *Training the Racehorse* (first published 1973), Tim Fitzgeorge-Parker considers the role of the jockey's *agent* with characteristic equanimity: 'A shabby little interloper, a totally unnecessary percentage spiv, who comes between the trainer and his rider, qualifying for the title of "the lowest form of animal life in racing".' In the twenty-first century *agents* are accepted as a fact of life, necessitated by the pressures of modern sport and facilitated by advances in mobile communication. Dave Roberts, who *books* rides for many of the leading jump jockeys is, for better and for worse, a more important individual figure in that *game* than many trainers. Major Fitzgeorge-Parker's opinion of *bloodstock agents* is unrecorded.

Ahead of the handicapper: A *progressive* horse not only keeps his **head in front** of his pursuers on the racecourse, but manages to stay *ahead of the handicapper* each time his performance is *assessed*: 'Make The Stand looks as if he might still be *ahead of the handicapper* and is one to *keep* very much *the right side of.*' The trick that connections must master to keep their horse *unexposed* is to ensure that the official winning distance of each victory is inversely proportional to the *amount in hand*.

Aids: 'Ballybrophy has *dropped like a stone* in the weights and much depends on whether a *first-time tongue-tie* can make a difference.' *Aids* in racing are not the same thing as **assistance**, which is usually given by the jockey. They are the inanimate devices *applied* to *help* a horse *concentrate*. The majority of these pieces of *equipment* have to be *declared* in advance by the trainer because a runner, particularly the *first time* he wears the *aid* in question, can be *transformed* and go like a **different horse**. Sadly, however, the so-called *aids* may turn out to be no help at all, as the continuation of the Ballybrophy story bears out: 'Tried just about all other *aids* available in the last 14 months.'

All day: The unit of measure for a horse's stamina, sometimes further amplified for effect: 'It's a tough race but he stays *all day long.*' *Forever*, or *forever and a day* are other mildly implausible estimations of how long a horse can **keep up** the gallop. Compare **every inch**.

All dressed up: 'As the race began to develop in earnest, Mulrennan on Blue Spinnaker was *all* *dressed up* but with *nowhere to go.*' Unfortunately for their backers, jockeys or horses described thus really do have *nowhere to go*, without a **split** that would give them a **passage**. They might run into a *wall* of horses, get *boxed in*, or be waiting for the *gap that never came.* A horse that was *all dressed up* might ultimately be described as an *unlucky loser*, but the less charitable on the Betfair forum might suggest that *the game* is b–nt or that the jockey *couldn't ride my missus.*

All out: A staple of potted race-reading, meaning 'under the strongest possible pressure to the line'. Pertains rather to the horses who win than to those who *just fail* or are *just held* (despite the fact that placed runners usually receive a similar amount of **assistance** from the saddle). Take this example of a close finish at Lingfield, where the summary comments for the winner are: 'Tracked leaders, going easily 2f out, shaken up and quickened to lead just inside 1f, driven and *all out.*' For the second: 'Tracked leader, ridden to lead briefly 1f out, chased winner after, ran on well near finish, *just failed.*' Race-readers are not paid to write prose as exciting as the races they describe, even if their concise style can generate a kind of poetry.

All over: When reporters note that a certain horse looked *all over* the winner, they are sure to be about to give the reasons why the horse did not actually win: 'The more prominently ridden Cherry Mix looked *all over* the winner when *looming up* alongside North Light two out, but Bago was now in *full* **cry** and *kept on* strongly to **collar** Cherry Mix close home.' However, during a race, commentators can use the same phrase when two horses are **upsides** to indicate that one is there only *on sufferance*: 'Harchibald is **cantering** *all over* Inglis Drever.'

Also ran: The phrase originated in racing, but its understated disdain was bound to carry its appeal beyond. National newspapers still tend to print the names of the first three runners home with the rest of the field listed under '*Also Ran:*'. But it is very rare for a professional to refer to an individual horse – before or after a race – as an *also-ran*: instead see *rags*, *washing*. The phrase *best of the rest*, common in pre-race analysis, seems hopeful but dismissive at one and the same time, while the rhyme may have a comforting effect.

Ambulance: 'After that first fence pile-up, there'll be *standing room only* in the *ambulance*.' As long as the commentator is fairly sure that no serious injuries have occurred, he may make a little joke about the jockeys getting a lift back to the *weighing room* in one of the two ambulances which are required to fol-low each race. Similarly, previews can describe a horse as an *early* or *last-fence casualty* in his previous outing, by now safe in the knowledge that no real harm was done. See also *walk home*.

Amiss: 'Dissident ran as if *something* were *amiss*.' This is the invariable expression if a horse runs *too bad to be true*, his performance being so poor that injury is the only likely explanation. More serious if the *something* is left out and the horse himself is so described: 'The Exeter race didn't *take much winning*, with a couple of the leading contenders running *as if amiss*.' More serious still if a commentator notes in running that a horse has gone *badly amiss*, in which case the injury may be bad enough for the *screens* to be erected.

Anchor: In handicaps, what a *hefty impost* or *welter burden* can do to a horse: 'Cloud Dancer was seemingly *anchored* by a big rise in the weights.'

Annihilate: Reserved for performances where the winner has left the rest *nowhere*: 'Hawk Wing *annihilated* his field at Newbury.' *Rout* and *murder* are alternatives. A less common usage is for chasers who *miss* a fence *out* and demolish its structure (sometimes so badly that it is *dolled off* next time round): 'And Stearsby has absolutely *annihilated* that open ditch.'

Any amount in hand: A standard piece of hyperbole to convey what a horse has *left in the tank* when completing a *facile* victory: 'Legal Right won *as he pleased* with *any amount in hand*' – so standard in fact that reporters can reach for even more amplified ways of saying an animal has *hacked* up: 'He won at Ripon with *any amount plus a bit more in hand*.'

Anything: 'He could be *anything*.' A phrase exuding optimism, used by countless connections when, on the basis of breeding, home work or early racecourse appearances, they weigh up the prospects of a relatively untried horse: 'Moayed could *develop* into *anything* next year on turf.' Usually it turns out that these horses *find nothing*.

Argument: 'Kausse de Thaix could never *get into the argument*.' This is a common narrative filler to mean a horse was not involved in the finish. Similarly, a frontrunner can try to *force the issue*, or *hold-up horses* can *join issue*. In some reports, *argument* can just mean the gallop, rather than the gallop at the end of a race: 'It Takes Time *sat* well off the *early argument*.' *In contention*, a phrase that crops up in many other sports, is used so routinely that it often loses all connotation of the contending parties being in an *argument*, although this may not be so true of the phrase *bang in contention*.

Armchair ride: 'Lester came in for an *armchair spare* ride on Shergar in the Irish Derby.' In other words, Lester could afford to sit **motionless**, as his horse never needed to *come off the bridle*. Denotes a win even *cosier* than a **steering job**.

Ask: 'When Tom Doyle *asked* Mendo the question, the *response* was immediate.' This does not of course mean that Mendo was quick on the buzzer, but that he *answered* his jockey's *urgings readily* when the race got **serious**. The relationship between horse and rider is often framed in terms of a question-and-answer session in this way, partly because the whip rules require a jockey to put his **stick** down if the horse is not *responding* to it: 'I kept *asking* for more and he a*nswered* all the way to the line.' More specifically, a jump jockey can *ask* his mount to *stand off* at a fence: 'Jodie has *asked* for a *big one* there but the horse has **put down** on him.'

Assert: Narrative shorthand for the moment when a horse is asked to show his *turn of foot* and *go on* from his field: 'Cauthen, who has a *clock in his head*, asked his mount to *assert* at just the right moment.' Impressive winners often *assert* in *good style*. The reflexive pronoun never seems to be required.

Assistance: A jockey is of course paid to *assist* his horse but this is the likely noun as soon as he is made to *assist* more imposingly: 'He just *got up* under *every assistance* from Pat Eddery'; 'In his last two wins Florida Pearl was given *considerable assistance* by Richard Johnson.' In these examples the qualifying adjective suggests the extent of the euphemism each time.

At it: 'Heltornic set a sound pace and had all her rivals *hard at it* a long way from home.' In other words the jockeys are *at* work because their mounts have come *off* the bridle. Indeed, if you are leaning over to a friend to remark that a frontrunner you've both backed has the rest of the field toiling, the phrases 'They're all *at it*' and 'They're all *off it*' are interchangeable (as are the various swearwords available when something then comes with a ***wet sail*** to ***touch*** *off* your selection on the line). When two horses are *locked in combat* you can also leverage up the expression in a fairly mechanised way: 'From the third last, down the hill and up the straight, Thomond and Golden Miller were *at it hammer and tongs*, until close home the Miller edged ahead.'

At the head of affairs: There are always runners who in the pre-race analysis *merit respect*. There are also those who in the race itself are a touch sensitive to their rightful status: 'Party Boss put in an impressive performance at Lingfield, since he was denied his favourite position *at the head of affairs*.' None can quite compare in the lexical hierarchy with the ***lord of all he surveys*** – just as long as the latter comes through with a *last-to-first* victory.

Attitude: References to *attitude* tend to be complimentary: 'Mogaamer has a *most likeable attitude* and has shown ***plenty*** of ***ability*** in his *prep work*.' But if a horse has a 'bad attitude', you are likely to find other ways of saying so, either blunt or euphemistic. See, for example, ***dog it*** and ***two ways of running***.

B

Back end: Frequently used by trainers when tracking the progress of their two-year-olds in the autumn, with *season* understood: 'He should win *his maiden* this *back end* and he'll be a nice prospect next season.' Much less common as a synonym for *quarters*: 'He didn't get his *back end* up and gave Carl no chance.' *Backside* might very occasionally be used in this context, but note that in North America it refers to the stable area at the racecourse rather than any area of equine anatomy.

Back for more: A phrase that recognises how a horse must be brave (or stupid) to respond *for pressure* in a race: 'Beau Ranger is nothing if not courageous and is coming *back for more*.' The same words can be employed when a horse is in the process of *running up* a *sequence*, particularly at one track: 'The Dark Lord is *back for more* after two course victories on good ground.' For the first usage, there are some colourful American versions: 'Bandini appeared to be a beaten horse in the Fountain of Youth Stakes, but he *re-broke* in deep stretch and finished *full of run* to be second to High Fly.'

Backhander: Jockeys are sometimes alleged to have received *backhanders* in return for not administering any in a particular race.

Back number: Operates only as a backhanded compliment: 'This run proved that Captains Table is *no back number*.' It would be far too categorical, a season or two later, to say that Captains Table actually was a *back number*; instead, you would find constructions such as 'He is finding it hard to *reproduce* his best form,' or 'He is not quite the *force of old*.'

Balloon: A metaphor for overjumping: 'Despite *ballooning* the first, his jumping was otherwise quick and accurate.' This is not quite as awkward as a *pogo-stick jump*, but it represents more of a mistake than simply giving an obstacle *plenty* of air.

Banker: While punters, connections and journalists usually have an idea of their *nap* of the day, the concept of the *banker* is reserved for a big meeting held over several days, when it identifies the one horse you'd get *stuck into* over all others: 'Our Vic would be my Cheltenham *banker* this season.' It is not unknown for funds to have run out before the *banker* has.

Barge: The requisite simile if a horse is *friendless* in the market: 'Sixo *drifted like a barge* in the ring but did nothing wrong in the race until falling at the fourteenth.' With runners who are being *given away*, so paper-thin is their support in the ring, you will occasionally hear a reference to their *drifting like the Kon-Tiki*.

Baton: This is *picked up* by a horse if he takes over the lead from another animal. The metaphor is rare, but apt when the previous leader *drops out* very *tamely*: 'When Knife Edge *put on the brakes* going out on the last circuit, Westender *picked up* the *baton* and made his bid for glory on the downhill run to two out.'

Beast: Horses become *beasts* at either end of the racing spectrum. During the hard hand-to-hand exchanges in the betting ring, punters can refer to horses as *beasts*, particularly when planning to have a monstrous bet on them: 'I'm *having it large* on the Sherwood *beast*.' By contrast, in the soft focus of television features showing slow-motion reruns of an emotional victory or images of a misty morning on the gallops, the voiceover will pay tribute to *man and beast* in *perfect harmony* – often accompanied by a few bars of Smetana or Mascagni for extra effect. This formulation is perhaps preferred because *horse and jockey* sounds like the name of a pub.

Beat: In the trade, this is by some way the more common form of the past participle: 'Norton's Coin from Toby Tobias, Dessie's toiling and he's *beat*!'; 'I got myself *beat* today by going too soon.' In the case of a horse, especially if well fancied, who trails in *well beat*, you may want to point out how few runners they had behind them at the finish: 'Mon Villez *beat* just one *home* in the Coral.'

Beater: One of the colloquial alternatives for whip, as in 'Young Derek Jacob's a bit *liberal* with the *beater*.' Considerably less euphemistic than ***persuader***.

Bedside manner: 'If a horse has run absolutely appallingly Carl will always help me and find something positive, and cheer the owners up. His *bedside manner* is second to none.' As a jumps jockey, Carl Llewellyn has no doubt ended up more in the hospital bed than by its side (for treatment to serious injuries after *crashing* falls), but the *bedside manner* he is being praised for here by his trainer is his ability to keep owners *sweet* in the somewhat more trying circumstances of a ***disappointing*** run by their horse.

Beholden: Racing sometimes provides a refuge for words otherwise seldom employed in current language. This one is trotted out when you are explaining that a horse is not *inconvenienced* by the ground: 'Doyen is not *beholden* to the state of the going, which gives connections a full range of races to aim at.' If this seems unduly formal, it is possible to talk of a horse that will *go on anything* or to whom *all types* of ground *come the same*.

Benefit: 'The four-miler at the Festival has been a Jonjo O'Neill *benefit* for the last three years'; 'The Champion Hurdle is threatening to become an Irish *benefit*.' In other words a certain race is ***farmed*** so successfully by certain connections or **raiders** that it seems they just have to *turn up* to *scoop* the pot. More occasionally, the word *benefit* can be used to indicate a very easy assignment for the favourite: 'One of the worst hunter chases for a long time, which amounted to nothing more than a *benefit* for Bengal Bullet, who only had to **stand up** to **collect**.'

Best work: 'First Of May was doing all his *best work* at the finish after having **plenty** *to do* from the turn.' A phrase which seems to be reserved for the *eyecatching* late effort of a horse who is running on at the death. Nobody ever seems to say that a front-runner who gets *reeled in* was doing all his *best work* at the start.

Between the flags: An acceptable way of referring to point-to-point racing because at these meetings, which are not *under rules*, flags rather than running rails can sometimes mark out the direction of the course. You may also see references to the *pointing field*, a term which betrays just the slightest sense that racing *between the flags* is an amateur and agricultural pursuit.

Big: The adjective for unfit horses and overgenerous odds (which may of course be related): 'He looks a bit *big* in the paddock and may need the run'; 'Rob Roy's double-figure price for the 2000 Guineas could look very *big* come May.' *Massive* is a synonym allowed in the latter context only. Horses can be praised for jumping *big and bold*, although if the *bold* is omitted the *big* is more likely to be a criticism, the implication being that the fences are being **ballooned**: 'Perhaps *reverting* to the smaller obstacles was an issue for Pleasure Shared, as he jumped a bit *big* today.' The *Big Red* was Phar Lap. The *Big Horse* was Mill House.

Birch: *Birch* can serve as an ersatz for fence: 'Strong
Flow resumes over fences more than a year after
he last *flew the birch* in earnest.' The *birch* is more
likely to be referred to directly when the fence
itself *flies* or is *parted* as the result of a **blunder**.
Remember to say *spruce* if commentating from
Aintree. *The big brown ones* is a more allusive way
of referring to steeplechases. We have seen rather
more exotic images: 'Lord Atterbury continues to
smash his way through the land's racing *foliage*.' The
smaller obstacles are referred to as *timber*, unless
they are *brush* hurdles of French origin. An individual hurdle is a *flight* – 'Four *flights* to jump . . .'
– although, especially in Ireland, the noun can be
used more generically: 'Given that was Lucky Star's
debut *over flights* he can be expected to improve
considerably.'

Bismarck: Popularised on *The Morning Line* by
Barry Dennis (at about the same time as you were
able to *lay* horses on the *exchanges*), the *Bismarck*
lends its name to the **jolly** thought likely to *go down*
in the race. The fact that this was a German ship
of course authorises the bookie's *Schadenfreude*
here, never mind whether she was actually scuttled
or not. But it may or may not be pertinent that in
the nineteenth century *Bismarcker* was a slang term
for a cheat at cards: certainly some *Bismarcks* over
the years will have been **nobbled** by the bookmakers.

Bits and pieces: Seen in two contexts, both relating
to outsiders for a race. First, when trying to argue a
case for them you can collect up *snippets* of evidence:
'He has *bits and pieces* of form round good tracks
and cannot be completely discounted.' There are variants: 'Algymo has the odd *strand* of form'; 'Indian
Pipe Dream has shown *glimmers* of **ability**.' Second,
if reporting on some market support, you can say

from the ring: 'There are *bits and pieces* for this
Shooting Light, who's into 10s.'

Black type: In sales catalogues, any placed performances in group or listed races are printed in bold
lettering (a winner earns capitals to boot). Trainers
the world over will therefore sometimes admit that
they are *going for* the *black type* when they aim a filly
or mare at such a race in the hope of *making the
frame*; other handlers focus less on an animal's
potential value in the *paddocks*: 'The *black type* on
offer over Brisbane's winter *carnival* is unlikely to
tempt trainer Gary Portelli to take improving filly
Chaud Roche north.'

Blanket finish: 'You could have thrown a *blanket* over
them.' This has become the standard way of visualising
the togetherness of the runners and riders involved in
a multiple burst for the line. In the case of the eight finishers with less than a length between them in the
2002 running of the Australian Newmarket Handicap,
it would have needed, apparently, a *tarpaulin*.

Blaze the trail: The phrase prompts visions of cowboys scorching across the Wild West, but on English
racecourses it offers a rather unspectacular alternative to the humdrum *set the pace*, as long as the pace
is a decent one: 'Not too many got into this, with
Little Ridge *blazing the trail* and only being **collared**
late on by Cashel Mead.' By the same token, *trail-
blazer* is one of the alternatives to *frontrunner* (what
cowboys who still like a bet might call a *speedball* or a
front-end player).

Blinder: A horse who runs very well, or above expec-
tations, can run a *blinder*, provided (perhaps curiously) that he doesn't actually win: 'He's run a
blinder to get so close to the winner after his *lay-off*

and I'm delighted.' *Screamer*, *cracker* and *corker* are
alternatives.

Blissfully unaware: Racehorses are usually cate-
gorised as *thinkers* or as creatures who are *daft as a
brush*. But, in ironic post-race mode, it is suddenly
appropriate to describe them as *blissfully unaware* of
the attention or opprobrium they are receiving. The
same phrase can also be used by those who believe
market moves are not necessarily an indicator of a
race's outcome: 'One thing's for sure, Holy Orders
himself is *blissfully unaware* he's *drifting* on the
exchanges.' It's probably a bit much then to surmise
that the derivation of the phrase is Hebrews 13:2,
even for this horse.

Blow his cover: A nice phrase that fits with the
dominant handicapping concept of being *exposed*
or *unexposed*: 'Farmer Jack looked *better than ever*
when *routing* his field at Aintree last time, but that
rather *blew his cover* and his *mark* has been adjusted
accordingly.'

Blowout: A *blowout* sounds quite dangerous, but it is
in fact a routine piece of home work or an easy prep
race, to ensure that a horse does not *blow up* on the
racecourse. Sometimes combined with the idea of
taking any excess *fizz* out of an animal: 'Considered
too *fresh* by Jessica Harrington last year, they have
given Moscow a little *blowout* at Punchestown before
this year's Festival.' There are other ways of describing
the same process: 'Appalachian Trail *cleared his lungs*
in the Lincoln Trial at Wolverhampton'; 'A *spin* on the
all-weather will have *blown away* the **cobwebs** for Wing
Commander's seasonal debut on turf.' Sometimes a
trainer will seek to provide evidence his charge did not
even *need the run*: 'We were delighted with him and he
wouldn't have *blown a candle out* after the race.'

Blow up: 'His first-time-out win was all the more
impressive given that he clearly *blew up* two furlongs
out but was *nursed* home.' Explosive as it may sound,
blow up is the canonical phrase for a horse who has
come to the end of his tether and failed to *see out* the
trip, usually because he was not at peak race fitness.

Blunder: A stock variant term, so that a 'last-flight
blunder' is not intended as being materially or stylis-
tically different from a 'last-fence *error*'. By contrast,
there is a degree of idiomatic life in the corresponding
verb: 'Havre De Thaix *blundered away* his chance
with a series of bad mistakes.'

Blunt: The standard verb if you are describing
attempts to draw the finishing kick out of **hold-up
horses**: 'Rubberdubber deserves extra credit being
the only *chasing type* in the field and in making the
running to try to *blunt* the flat performers' speed.'
When it comes to the adjective, the trainers who are
described as *blunt* by newspapers edited in London
often seem to be based north of the Trent.

Boards: When a horse is *backed off the boards* his price
is being **slashed**. It is always a moment that boosts our
egos when we find an outlying price *in a **place*** and our
bet causes a bookie to *wipe* the price *off* his *board*. But
the feeling of triumph is usually short-lived, either
because we realise the layer was in fact petrified by the
legendary punter standing directly behind us, or when
he writes up a new price which is even longer. If you
back a horse *across the board*, you will be in the United
States and placing three *wagers* on a horse to *win*, *place*
and *show* (the *handle* for each *pool* is displayed on the
infield *Tote board*). The plural is never seen there unless
an illegal bookmaker is operating.

Boat: The *boats* racing people seem to be thinking of

when they use this simile are large and difficult to
manœuvre – oil tankers rather than launches: 'Envopak
Token is as slow as a *boat*.' If the ground becomes too
firm for these *staying types*, the *boat* duly *drifts* like a
barge in the ring if still allowed to *take its chance*.

Bobber: Commentator's vernacular for a very close
finish which will be decided *on the nod*: 'They're still
absolutely neck and neck, *locked in combat* right to
the line, it's a *bobber*!'

Boggy: *Weighing-room* vernacular for a jockey who
is not particularly **stylish** or *polished*: 'Andy was
exceptionally *boggy* when he started and, while he is
as neat as he can be today, his *style* remains unique.'
The adjective may derive from words such as *bogger*
and *bogtrotter* which the English would level at
Irish immigrants, but, given the enduring success of
Irish jockeys, the connection seems tenuous to say
the least.

Bold bid: If you read an observation like 'Dun Locha
Castle made a *bold bid* from the front,' you know you
are about to hear why Dun Locha Castle did not
prevail. The same is true of top-weights who make a
bold bid to *defy* the handicapper.

Bollocking: The invariable *mot juste* when a trainer
tells anybody off. Used particularly by jockeys recount-
ing stories of their youth, when their boss was *hard
but fair*: 'The Duke always supported you, but you
could guarantee a *right bollocking* if you went against
orders.' *Right rollocking* is the alliterative and bowdlerised version, not usually required in these more per-
missive times. A *rig* is a horse with at least one *rollock*
retracted, although horses like Selkirk have proved that
this is no barrier to performing well on the racecourse
and at stud.

Bolt: While it is not good news to hear of a horse *bolting* at home, in the paddock, going down to or at the start of a race, it is much better news at the *business end* of the contest: 'He's absolutely *bolted up* with *any amount in hand*'; 'He was taking a *step up* in class but has still *bolted in.*'

Bombproof: A way of saying a horse is absolutely *sound* in limb or mind, or that nobody in his *grade* can undermine him, or that he is a *stone-cold* certainty for a particular race. Sometimes all these ideas are present: 'Judged on his very *slick* jumping in the Gowran *trial*, Hardy Eustace looks *bombproof* for the Champion Hurdle.' While *bombproof* horses have still been known to *blow up* in a race (Americans call shock winners *bombs*), you would not expect their temper to explode in the *preliminaries*, whatever the provocation: 'Dancing Brave is absolutely *bombproof*. If someone chucked a handgrenade over the rail during the parade he wouldn't bat an eyelid.'

Bonus: 'Anything he does over hurdles is a *bonus.*' The mantra when you are training *chasing types*. The insider's retranslation might well read loosely as follows: 'Anything this *boat* does over hurdles will be an *effing* miracle. He's so *effing* slow the only possible chance he has of winning is in a 3m 6f hunter chase round *effing* Chepstow.' Flat trainers can, more occasionally, speak in the same terms about a two-year-old's season: 'If he picks up a *little* race at the *back end*, that's a *bonus.*'

Boot on: Alternative to *kick on*, which is so common it means 'accelerate' without punters needing to think what the jockey is doing with his feet: 'Richard Johnson *boots* Palarshan *on* into the lead now.' *Boot home* is the recurrent phrase for a finishing run, and it boils down, in effect, to being synonymous with 'win': 'Mercer has since *booted home* another two dozen winners.' We note also the slogan for a betting service provider in Australia which invites you to join vicariously in the action: '*Boot home* a winner with me.'

Bottomless: Acts in racing parlance as the superlative of *soft*, although it is possible to amplify even this: 'He wants *absolutely bottomless* ground'; 'We'd have to pull him out if it came up *really bottomless*.' Trainers can also talk about getting to the *bottom* of a horse's **ability** or fitness, and not wanting to *bottom* a young horse too soon.

Bounce factor: It is an accepted fact that horses who come back from a long lay-off succumb to the *bounce factor*. In other words, they **shape** promisingly or even win on their reappearance, but then **disappoint** on their second run: 'Blazing Walker suffered from the *bounce factor* here after that good placed effort the other week.' The verb form is also available: 'D J Flippance has come out of the race in great form, but as he had been off for 876 days before that I'm scared he will *bounce*.' This always means 'bounce down' rather than 'bounce back', which can be confusing to students of other markets.

Bowl along: 'Keepthedreamalive enjoyed being allowed to *bowl along* in front.' Horses so allowed are running pretty *free*, but not necessarily impairing their chances of winning, because they are not **pulling** *for their heads*. Enthusiastic **sorts** not permitted to *bowl along* (or, in a nice synonym, *lob along*) are very often **disappointed**.

Boys: 'I left some of my money with *the boys* at Cheltenham.' The words of the **legendary** J. P. McManus, referring to the bookies who had temporarily filled their **satchels** at his expense, mix familiarity with contempt. A *boy* is an apprentice or otherwise inexperienced jockey, especially in Australia: 'The horse threw the *boy* and was not allowed to take part.' But lady jockeys always seem to be called *girls* whether or not they are being thrown out of the saddle.

Break: Commentators can either remark on an *even break* or notice that a horse has *missed the break* at the start of a race, particularly on the flat out of starting stalls. There are alternatives for the latter circumstance: 'Makabul *missed the beat* but recovered impressively' (see also *fall out of the stalls*). Once they have *jumped off*, it is slightly more difficult to gauge a phrase such as 'Then there's a *break* of seven lengths or so to the remainder.' Often this is just routine commentary, perhaps provoked by having to move the binoculars in order to get sight of the next group of runners, but the phrase can indicate the race-caller's belief that the *chasing **pack*** has become *detached*.

Breast: If you are an athlete, *breasting* the tape is advisable, and if you are a footballer *chesting* the ball is part of good control. But these verbs are used of **equine** *athletes* when they have, less commendably, *got low* at a fence: 'The 4/9 favourite *breasted* a few of the early obstacles'; 'I've *chested* the second last but got away with it.'

Breeze: A *breeze* is a light canter – 'All being well I'll *breeze* him the Saturday before the race' – and so an easy winner can *breeze* home. In *breeze-up sales* the animals are therefore put through their easier *paces* so that potential buyers can examine their **actions**: '"She's an athletic, racy filly who *breezed* really well and Pivotal is *doping* brilliantly," said Anthony Stroud, an advisor to Sheikh Rashid.'

Bridle: The most important piece of equipment worn by any horse but particularly crucial for a rider trying to control half a ton of thoroughbred. Whether a horse is *on* or *off the bridle* is the most classic indicator of how well he is *travelling*. Hence the number of colourful ways to describe these two states, because the moment in a race when a runner goes from being **hard on the steel** to *spitting out the bit* is the moment of truth. If he *finds* **nothing**, he will be described as a *bridle horse*, a term that is usually pejorative.

Broken down: The canonical euphemism for serious tendon damage, which will often end a horse's career unless remedies such as *firing*, artificial implants or a year or two *out in a field* are successful: *'I'm afraid he's broken down* on his off fore and it doesn't look very good at all.' While the customary analogy of the motor car may be present in the phrase, it may also hint at the reaction of connections when they hear the news.

Buck: A substitute for **stag**, especially if the horse is a novice: 'Ashley Brook is jumping like a *buck.'* *Bucking and kicking*, unless it happens in the starting stalls when it would constitute a serious piece of bad **manners**, tends to be a sign of rude health: 'She's been *tearing up* the gallops and was *bucking and kicking* this morning when I fed her.'

Buckle end: 'David Crosse was at the *buckle end* there.' *Of the rein* is always understood in this phrase, which is used when a jockey survives a **blunder**. He may or may not actually have done so by holding tight to the knot he tied in his reins before the race started.

Bullfinch: If you go to watch jump-racing in France, *bullfinch* is probably the only word you'll pick out when straining to understand the excitable on-course commentary. Perhaps the French, who use the word to denote a rather huge fence, don't realise that the British use it to denote a rather small bird.

Bumper: Flat races run under National Hunt rules designed to educate *store* horses. The probable derivation is that these races used to be confined to *boggy* amateurs who *bump* up and down in the saddle. Some yards specialise with their *bumper horses*: 'Noel Chance's runners always deserve respect in this *sphere*.' *Bumping and boring* are more likely to be reported in a competitive flat race.

Bunch: As in: 'Haslam is a well known as a *"bunch" trainer* – when the horses are in form you can suddenly expect him to *fire in* a load of winners.' Otherwise, although a field can *bunch together*, this phrase is used less than in cycling or athletics, and less in the British Isles than the United States.

Buried: 'He got it all wrong at the ditch and absolutely *buried* me.' This is a term in jump jockeys' vernacular which is rarely seen in print unless a journalist quotes a rider. An example of the gallows humour prevalent in the *weighing room*.

Burlington Bertie: Rhyming slang for 100/30, often abbreviated to *Burlington*, derived from the Edwardian music-hall song performed by Vesta Tilley. Another example of rhyming slang for particular odds is *Major Stevens* for even money (also known as *levels you devils*). See *exes* for examples of backslang. *Carpet*, for 3/1, evolves from *carpet bag*, criminals' cant for a three-month jail term (the length of time it supposedly took for a prison workshop to produce a regulation-size carpet). But note that *double carpet* means not 6/1 but 33/1.

Burst: Used pejoratively of a jockey who *makes* too much *use* of a horse early in a race, or of a trainer who gets to the ***bottom*** of his ***inmates*** too impatiently: 'It was a bad ride from the ***boy*** and the horse was *burst* before the ***business end***'; 'Always a doubt surrounding fitness on seasonal reappearance and Hills is not one for *bursting* his horses early doors.' Perhaps there is an extra resonance in that *bleeders* – by which we mean horses who *burst* blood vessels rather than characters in the ring – ***stop*** *to nothing* very quickly.

Business end: 'City Affair was ***one-paced*** *at the business end*'; 'Parasol is a tough cookie who should be there or thereabouts *at the business end.*' If Parasol finishes there rather than thereabouts, he could be said to *do the business*. Big Ron rides again, it would seem.

Buy money: A term for betting long-odds-on with the implication that the favourite is certain to ***collect***, so that the wager is the equivalent of a short-term deposit at much higher interest rates than those available in the high street. The *exchanges* have also made it possible for *pyjama traders* to lay horses at *massive* prices. However, *buying money* in this way often proves to be a ***mug***'s ***game***: 'Only the person who laid the biggest bet on Betfair (£25 at 1,000) on Kicking King will know whether he *took his medicine* and *covered* himself at shorter, but he might not be trying to *buy money* again for a while.' An American who tries such strategies risks being called a *bridge jumper* (particularly apt if he has been *show plunging*), whereas losing odds-on punters elsewhere have to be imagined as *throwing themselves* from the *top of the stands*.

C

Cabbage patch: A course marred by *false* ground or an uneven covering of grass can attract this dismissive label. A signature phrase of François Doumen when referring to the heavily watered Parisian jumps tracks: 'It's true my *fellow* struggled last time but Auteuil is little more than a *cabbage patch*.'

Cajole: 'Dettori *cajoled* one last *call* from the game five-year-old.' *Coax* and *conjure* are other available terms when a final thrust is required. More typically, though, *cajoling* (see also **niggle**) registers the work that the rider may have to do through the whole course of a race. The following example runs the gamut of the lexicon in its attempt to simulate the jockey's efforts to out-think his horse all the way: 'Not for nothing is John McNamara the champion amateur in Ireland, as he showed when *kidding, cajoling, finessing* and occasionally *bullying* his enigmatic mount to *reel in* Luzcadou.' No doubt the enigmatic mount, called Spot Thedifference, was able to distinguish the shades of meaning intimately.

Call: If there is a photo finish, it falls to the *judge* to *call* the placings, so when you're in a betting shop and hear over the *blower* that a horse has been *called third* you know that this is the official result. The usage is less 'official' in an example like 'He could be *called* the winner a long way out,' where the judgement is likely to have come from the racecourse commentator. *Call* is in any case a synonym for 'commentate': 'Simon Holt will be the man *calling* them home today.'

Call a cab: 'Brian Harding was the jockey *calling a cab* at that ditch.' The expression not only brilliantly visualises the action of a jockey trying to keep his balance when his mount overjumps and he takes one hand off the reins, but perhaps also cruelly implies that he might well need a safer *conveyance* such as a taxi to get him *home*. Trotted out with particular relish by English commentators when an overseas rider such as Jacques Ricou *calls a cab*. *Waving to the crowd* is an equally ironic way of putting it, especially on a wet weekday at Wincanton.

Call a few names: 'Batswing has been *called a few names* in the past, but Gary Moore insists he is one of the most *genuine* horses in training.' This is a likely formula for a horse who does not necessarily *go through with* his *effort*, to the disappointment of connections and punters. Most racehorses do of course have more than one name, but neither of them is likely to be uttered in these circumstances.

Came to grief: A very common way of saying 'to fall', usually followed by the location of the mishap: 'Redemption was going well until he *came to grief* at the first one down the back.' You would not use this expression for a fall where *grief* really did ensue.

Camp jockeys: The Harry Enfield sketches where a pair of effete riders did a lot of talking but not much racing has come into punters' vernacular to describe an *armchair ride*: 'Did you see how easily Hedgehunter won? It was *camp jockeys* at the Elbow.'

Canter: Derived from the *Canterbury pace*, the gait in between the trot and the gallop, both quick enough to ensure that you looked keen to arrive at the place of pilgrimage and slow enough to ensure some overnight stays in taverns on the journey. But if a horse is said to be *cantering* in the *closing stages* of a race *under* *rules*, he is likely to win *easily*, especially if ***travelling*** at a ***hack*** *canter*. See also ***all over***.

Card: For each meeting racecourses produce an official *racecard*, and that *card* stands as a metonym for the whole day: 'It's a cracking little *card* at Ponty.' Tipsters, punters, trainers and jockeys all try to *go through* the *card* by winning each race, although instances like Dettori's *Magnificent Seven* at Ascot are extremely rare. Curiously, the obligatory phrase when a trainer wins races on the same day at different racecourses, although there are obviously separate *cards* for each meeting, always uses a singular form: 'General Gossip set up a quickfire *across-the-card* double for Richard Phillips, completed minutes later by The Mick Weston over at Chepstow.' *Marking your card* with your own or other people's tips is a long-standing practice and the phrase has gone into the language.

Care: Many people working in the racing industry do have deep emotional ties to the animals they look after, but in racing parlance the word *care* forms part of a periphrasis for 'trained by': '*Under* Martin Pipe's *care*, Unsinkable Boxer has improved dramatically.'

Careless: *Careless* riding is carefully defined in the rule book as 'causing ***interference*** by inattention'. It is obviously less cavalier than *reckless* riding, but note that journalists would never use either term to describe jockeyship that was really *careless* or *reckless*, unless such riding had come to the attention of the stewards.

Car keys: Not the most common phrase when comparing a horse to a vehicle, but memorable in this example where Paul Nicholls is scratching his head about the lifeless performances of an expensive purchase at the

northern sales: 'When we bought Garruth we must
have left the *car keys* in Doncaster.'

Carry: *Horsemen* can confide that an animal *carries
himself* well and, unless there is an obviously high or
low *head carriage*, we take their word for it. Some
horses *carry* weight better than others: the *classier* ones
can be lined up for a great *weight-carrying* performance
or deliberately kept away from handicaps by their
trainers: 'I want to keep Regal Roller to *weight-for-age*,
otherwise he will *carry the grandstand.*' A horse *carried
out* by another runner is not a stretcher-case but will
inevitably find itself *out of the **frame***.

Carry his cross: 'Poor old Rooster Booster was
forced, not for the first time this season, to *carry his
own cross.*' Even though it may sound as though the
horse was running without the **assistance** of a
jockey, let alone Simon of Cyrene, or that he was toiling under the burden of top weight, these suggestions
are secondary. The metaphor is supposed to emphasise how heavy a task it can be to *cut out* your own
running. The handicapper may well duly *crucify* the
horse with a big *hike* in the ratings if he is not already
clobbering him.

Catch a tartar: It was rotten luck for highwaymen
when their prospective victims robbed them. In these
circumstances, they apparently *caught a tartar*. Now,
when horses are said to *catch a tartar*, they do not
actually catch the winner, but are unlucky enough to
come up against an animal who has not been **exposed**
for what he is: 'It transpires that Master Beveled
caught a real *tartar* when beaten by Make A Stand in
the William Hill.' The use is especially apt in valuable
handicaps where the connections of the placed horses
have the big prize snatched away from them by a
coup even better planned than their own.

Catch me if you can: Words attributed by the commentator to jockeys who attempt to *make all* or kick
on with a sudden and decisive injection of *pace*: 'And
Frankie says *catch me if you can* as he *presses the button* two out.' The phrase can be imputed even more
imaginatively to the horse itself: 'Enemy Action, setting off in his characteristic *"catch-me-if-you-can"*
style.' Sometimes, in the heat of battle, a victorious
jockey can make taunting hand gestures to his rivals
to similar effect: Christophe Soumillon on Dalakhani
in the Prix du Jockey Club and Paul Carberry on Beef
Or Salmon in the Lexus are two recent examples.

Catch pigeons: Unduly bullish trainers, or tipsters
claiming to be *in the know*, might reckon that a particular horse has been moving fast enough in his home
work to warrant this improbable image: 'My *contact*
tells me that Katie Nowaitee has *literally* been *catching
pigeons* on the *gallops* and rates a 100 point *maximum
bet* today for my followers.' A trainer like Malcolm
Jefferson has been around long enough to realise that
such exploits can count for little: 'Roman Art is not the
quickest horse *at home* but those who *catch pigeons* on
the *gallops* don't catch anything on the racecourse.'

Catch right: 'Idaho d'Ox is not easy to *catch right*,
but he *shaped* encouragingly in a keeping-on fourth.'
If a horse tends to have *two ways of running* or is
difficult to *prepare*, this is one way of saying that he
needs everything to *pan out* to win.

Cavalry charge: Used of sprint handicaps with a big
field or indeed of any race where a *blanket finish* is
expected: 'The presence of Rhinestone Cowboy in
last season's Coral Cup meant we were not treated
to the usual *cavalry charge* approaching the final
flight.' If the early pace is *suicidal*, comparisons to the
Charge of the Light Brigade are foreseeable.

Chain reaction: Nice little phrase for the not-so-nice moment when a falling horse brings down another, who in turn brings down or hampers other runners: 'Of the others to depart in the *chain reaction*, Another Deckie and Riders Revenge were still *in the mix* at the time.'

Change: It is no surprise that jockeys *change* their *hands* and horses *change* their *legs*. The former phrase describes the rider altering his length of rein, as the commentator notes what will sometimes turn out to be a first **distress signal**: 'Michael just *changing his hands* there on the favourite.' Nor is a horse *changing his legs* a good sign, as the fact that he is *leading* with the other foreleg suggests he is not **handling** the *turns* or the *ground*, or that something is **amiss**.

Change of scenery: A *change of scenery* really means 'a change of trainer', particularly when an improvement in the horse's form ensues: 'Arctic Blue changed stables since his last outing and clearly the *change of scenery* had a very positive effect.' The figure minimises, without entirely allaying, the suggestion that the horse was moved because the owners had fallen out with the previous handler, or that the improved form results from different *training methods*.

Cherry-ripe: It seems that only this fruit is allowed when you are looking for a metaphor to say you have your horse *spot on*: 'Petite Margot ran superbly last weekend after a break and I hope that will have left her *cherry-ripe* for this.'

Choke: The metaphor for losing under pressure is particularly apposite in racing, where horses can indeed **stop** very quickly after *swallowing* their *tongues*. But the word is more commonly seen in a motoring allusion to indicate that a horse is probably too *free*: 'Golden Crusader is certainly running with the *choke out* in the early stages.'

Clear: *Drew clear* is the race-reader's shorthand for 'got so far in front that nobody would catch him'. This is the point where, live in running, an Australian commentator may tell the crowd that he has *put down the glasses*, because the result is so clear-cut. Earlier in a race what constitutes a *clear lead* is a more fluid concept, but when told that a group of horses is *clear* of the *remainder* you should not expect anything in the *remainder* to be winning.

Clip: Synonym for *pace*, always a fast one: 'They went a really good *clip* from *flagfall*.' Used of home work as well as races: 'Led up by a stable companion, North Light worked at a reasonable *clip*.' May derive from the fast ships, unless you think that in a fast gallop, rather than a trot, there is a lot more *clip* than clop.

Clobber: Neither applicable to over-exuberant jockeys, nor even to chasers prone to **blunders**, but the verb indicates what the handicapper is likely to do to you if you win too *readily*: 'We'll probably get *clobbered* for this win so we may have to plan a quick reappearance.' There are some lively variants to be found as well, which make it sound as if the draconian *assessor* deserves a whip ban himself: 'The handicapper *whacked* him up a stone for completing the hat-trick.'

Close enough: If there is a short-priced favourite or **talking horse** in the race, a commentator will keep a special eye out for him and inform punters, if said horse is still *on the bridle* as they begin to *get **serious***, that he is *close enough*, or in the full version, *close enough if good enough*. See also **Here comes**.

Cobwebs: 'Wing Commander *collected* over a mile at Pontefract in August and has had a prep on the *all-weather* to blow away the *cobwebs*.' Horses seem to get enmeshed in *cobwebs* surprisingly quickly and so periodically need *freshening up*, and perhaps having a *blow* after the race.

Collar: 'Sun Bird made good late ground but was never going to *collar* Landing Light on the run-in.' In our experience this is the most common verb for catching the leader near the finish, but *reel in* and *nail* also come into the frame. The basis for the metaphor is perhaps least clear in the case of *collar*, but it seems legitimate to imagine a felon being apprehended from behind by the long arm of the law. In which case, *close home*, the usual phrase in attendance, fits suggestively.

Collect: The verb attributes to a winning horse the subsequent action of the successful connections and punters. It can therefore simply mean 'win' in a narrative context: 'Culloty was in the saddle when Matt Sheppard's *charge collected* last month at Huntingdon.'

Coltish: While instances of sexed-up colts (*entire* horses four years old or younger) actually trying it on with a filly at the racecourse are rare, an excess of testosterone leads to other kinds of *coltish behaviour* which are not recommended: being *on your toes*, getting *worked up* in the *preliminaries*, and generally being *headstrong* and difficult. If a colt is not *classy* (and therefore with little potential value at stud) and persists in such behaviour, he will probably find that he is a *gelding* sooner rather than later, even if no jumping career is envisaged for him. Sometimes *colty types* seem to get the message: 'We threatened Elkhorn with an *appointment at the vets* and he ran much better at Newmarket.'

Come: As with many common verbs, the meaning in racing is largely dependent on the accompanying preposition. *Come for* is the most common phrase in betting-ring vernacular to indicate heavy support that makes a horse's price *come in*: 'They've really *come for that* Joes Edge – the **Burlington** has all gone and he's *in* to 3s.' You can use *come in* for a second time if the gamble is duly *landed*: 'Monocle *came in* at an *SP* of 3/1'. Here is another example with two phrasal verbs, relating this time to training: 'Clan Royal *came back* in late but Jonjo is happy with him. It is nice to get him out again but he will *come on* for the run.' **Come back** has *into training* and *out of the field* both understood (see also the separate entry for an in-running usage), while *come on* is a ubiquitous phrase for how a horse's fitness will improve *for* a race or sharp *piece of work*. Finally, there is a little phrase trainers use when trying to predict conditions underfoot: 'I'm worried the ground will *come up* too quick for him at Ludlow.'

Come back: 'Long-time leader Quick is *coming back* to his field.' In reality the field are *running* the leader *down*, but because of their respective speeds this is the way a commentator would put it. Sometimes a horse *running on* from off the pace – by luck or judgement – finds that everything comes right: 'Last year's hero Amberleigh House found the race *coming back* to him with a late **faller** and a non-stayer in front.'

Come too soon: 'Perhaps in hindsight the race *came a bit soon* for him'; 'My only concern is it might *come too quickly* after his win at Kilbeggan.' Jockeys are sometimes criticised for *coming* (or *going*) *too soon* but as common is this rather disingenuous form of words used by beaten or nervous trainers. After all, they are the people who know the **programme book** and have decided to run a horse in an upcoming race, rather than the appointment at the racecourse having unavoidably stolen up on the poor unsuspecting animal. A defence might be that, given the *opportunities* available, connections had *nowhere else to go*, but they probably knew in their hearts they were *going to the well* once too often.

Come to win his race: Like other expressions in race-reporting (see **all over**, **process**), a phrase that sets up the revelation that something else happened: 'Two furlongs out Bering made his move on the outside and *came to win his race*, only to be *scythed down* by Dancing Brave's well-timed run.'

Company: You can judge a horse not least by the *company* he or she keeps: 'Dusky Warbler is expected to take on *better company* after gaining experience'; 'Eva So Charming should give a good account from the front in this less *exalted company*.' Leaders of a race who have been *out on their own* for too long appreciate *company* of any kind, except perhaps that of loose horses: 'He was **idling** a bit in front because he had led for such a long time and just needed some *company*.' Compare **splendid isolation**.

Competitive: In other words, able at least to *get into* the **argument** of a race. Seen more often than not when a journalist is noting that a horse will not or has not done so: 'It's hard to see him being *competitive* off that mark in such a *hot race*'; 'After leading in the early stages, Bob's The Business was unable to *get competitive* on the final circuit.'

Compressed: A word used to qualify handicap races when the *marks* of the highest- and lowest-weighted horses are within the maximum and minimum weights as set out in the conditions of the race: 'The National seems to get more *compressed* by the year, with Le Coudray rated 155 and the last horse to **get**

in running *off* 134.' *Compressed* handicaps are usually *ultra-competitive*, in contrast to those where a very highly rated top weight puts most of the other runners *out of the handicap*.

Concert pitch: A rare expression, probably connected with the conceit that horses are **tuned** *up* by their trainers, to describe a horse at the very peak of fitness or not, as the case may be: 'After his long *lay-off*, Ned Kelly won't be at *concert pitch* first time out.'

Condition: This is the *paddock watcher*'s way of saying that a horse is 'fat' (approximations are *burly* and *gross*). Usually seen when it is acknowledged the horse will *need the run*: 'Lo Stregone was *carrying condition* and there was definitely something left to *work on*.' But it can also be used, tongue-in-cheek, of humans, especially retired jockeys who *waste* no longer: 'Terry seems to be *carrying* a little bit more *condition* than in his riding days.'

Confirmed: For some reason, front runners are very often *confirmed*. *Habitual* is another qualifier, which makes them sound like criminals rather than Christians or bachelors.

Conformation: Although nobody ever seems to get round to explaining it, there does seem to be a concept *paddock-side* (or, more pertinently, sales-ring side) of the horse with perfect *conformation*, the kind of animal that is said to *fill the eye*. But often the word can turn out to be a synonym for *soundness*: 'Lots of people turned him down on *conformation* but I liked him anyway.' Mark Johnston is one shrewd judge of horseflesh who has little time for the skills or the jargon of some *bloodstock agents*: 'There are too many idiots out there who try to break it down – it's *toes in* or *toes out*, it's *back at* the knee or *over at* the knee. You can't do that.'

Connections: A key word whose scope depends on the context. In its widest sense, it really does mean everybody *connected* with the horse, from the owner down to the stable lad, along with the mother-in-law of the first cousin of the assistant trainer's wife. Photographs of the winning *connections* can therefore include many people (including, particularly for Irish winners at Cheltenham before increased security was introduced, hundreds of *connections* of the *connections*). In a different situation the range of reference can narrow down to a horse's legal owners and give a hint of the tension beyond the yard: 'I didn't want to put him in the race but the *connections* were keen to see him run on a London track.' On the other hand, if an owner likes a bet and his trainer likes to *plot one up*, they can be seen as close allies: 'Fontanesi's *wily connections* were no doubt less shocked by his win in the last than the majority of the crowd.' Or again, *connections* can be *sporting* if the owner persuades the trainer (or the trainer persuades the owner) to run in a handicap with a *welter burden*, or in a big race overseas. Of course journalists sometimes make a formulaic reference to *connections* when they have forgotten the trainer's name or have no clue as to the identity of the lady in the big hat collecting the owner's trophy. Nevertheless, the term remains a resonant word in the lexicon, in that it reflects not only the emotional *connection* between humans and animal, but also, for all that, the social connotation of being *well connected*.

Continue: 'The only other ones *continuing* are Pat Alaska and Solares.' Commentators will look back down the field to remind the crowd who, *technically*, is still *in* the race. Horses so described should really be pulled up, but their jockeys are carrying on in the hope of picking up some place money or a lower handicap mark. So whenever you hear your selection is *continuing* it is time to ***rip up your slip***. Similarly, when horses are *relegated to last*, they will not be winning unless the entire field *does a Devon Loch*.

Conveyance: Rather a sardonic alternative for 'horse', given that the implication is whether a particular animal's jumping is *safe* or not: 'Hacifal is a more *reliable conveyance* and looks the one to beat.'

Corkscrew: One of those mimetic terms in racing that describes a style of jumping where the horse twists in midair. This will not necessarily cause him to *come to grief*, but it may suggest that something is ***amiss*** or that he has *lost his bottle*.

Coughing: Aside from losing horses *in action*, two of the worst moments that happen in a trainer's routine are when he feels *heat* in the legs of one of his horses (as luck would have it, almost always his best one) or when he hears one of them *cough*. *Coughing in the yard* is the formula to cover any bug or fever that is laying ***inmates*** low and that may even cause the ***shutters*** to go up. If the health reports concern a star horse, the bulletins can be quite detailed, as in this report by Henrietta Knight on Best Mate: 'He *gave some coughs* last night, and this morning when we fed him he *gave some coughs* after that.'

Country: The section of a racecourse circuit furthest away from the stands, which prompts this ready commentating filler: 'So they *go out into* the *country* on the second circuit . . .' This part of the course is often where the race is said to be *won or lost*. Almost always used of jumps tracks – at Aintree the *country* is so extensive that a team of commentators is required to ***call*** the action – although the phrase can lend itself for an unfamiliar start to a long-distance flat race like the Cesarewitch (which actually starts in

another *county*). The phrase is less likely to be heard
at the more *metropolitan* tracks, but commentators
there may yet be seduced by fantasies of a rural idyll,
just as the new imagined venues for **virtual** greyhound racing – Brushwood, Millersfield – seem to
have transferred the dogs from their traditional urban
locations.

Coup: Usually qualified by *handicap*, in tribute to the
military precision with which connections can line
up a *good thing*: 'Another *handicap coup* by Captain
Price as his filly leaves all her previous form behind.'
See also **plot** and **touch**.

Cover: *Cover*, the technical term in breeding for
'shag', means something else at the racetrack – at
least we hope so: 'Dave got him *covered up* today and
gave him a brilliant ride.' *Cover* is essential for **hold-
up horses** who need to *come late* and will run *too free*
if they see **daylight** early in the race. You will therefore hear observations in commentary such as 'Dale
is looking for some *cover* so he can *switch* the favourite
off', or 'Rodrigo de Triano is nicely *covered up*'. There
obviously comes a point in the race – a very late
point for horses who **doss** *in front* – when *cover* can
become **traffic**. The past participle can serve to indicate that a horse will not be **run down** by another:
'Yankeedoodledandy was second after making a bad
mistake at the last, but had the rest well *covered*.'

Crab: A colloquialism meaning 'to find fault with' by
no means confined to racing, but the *OED* classifies
it as *stable-talk*: 'Draw analysts will *crab* his *berth* in
17'; 'A lot of people will be queueing up to *crab* the
favourite.' The noun appears in a simile for a horse who
could not be said to be enjoying the **preliminaries**: 'He
went down to post like a *crab*.'

Crawl: 'They're *crawling along* in the early stages.' This is the likely verb when there is no early pace *on*. But later, if a horse is said to be *creeping closer* – a metaphor connected to the idea of *stealthy progress* – he will probably be going pretty fast.

Credentials: These represent a horse's whole case history from its *bloodlines* through its previous track record down to its current form and *wellbeing*. Consequently, money is not the only thing at stake when they are presented in the course of duty: 'Moscow Flyer puts his considerable *credentials* on the line at Punchestown'; 'With a weight allowance and an apparent fitness advantage Well Chief appeared to have a stage to advertise his *credentials* for the Queen Mother.'

Credit: 'Solerina, like Limestone Lad before her, is a *tremendous credit* to her connections'; 'The *tough* and *genuine* Take The Stand reflects *great credit* on the Bowen yard.' Such standard phrases seem rather unfair to the horses themselves, who often appear to get no recognition for the qualities of toughness and durability being praised. The expression always seems to be used of very *straightforward* horses (or occasionally very good-looking ones). When handlers manage to coax a less *genuine* animal into putting his *best foot forward*, never say that the horse is a *credit* to connections but instead extol a *great feat* of training.

Cruise: Commonly employed in running commentary to denote a horse going well *within himself* on the bridle: 'Harchibald is absolutely *cruising* in behind the leaders.' Trainers and jockeys will often wax lyrical about an animal's high *cruising speed*, always a sure sign that the horse will *travel* well in his races. It has also been known for a jockey to press the *cruise-control button* if he is winning with *plenty in hand*.

Cry: Trainers are always complaining that their
horses cannot speak to them, but they sometimes seem
to receive a loud enough message from previous runs:
'His handler feels that Obay is *crying out* for three
miles'; 'With that **action** he seems to be *crying out* for
a softer surface.' The same idea can be expressed with
more extravagant hyperbole: 'Royal Paradise galloped
all the way to the line in a **manner** that *screamed* Royal
& Sun Alliance Hurdle.' When a horse obviously
has no more to give in a race he can be said to have
cried enough, whereas if a horse and jockey are sum-
moning up a charge in the closing stages, they are
described as *in full cry* (the jockey may indeed be
bawling encouragement).

Cut: 'The unkindest *cut* proved a recipe for success
for Barathea Dreams in the Spring Mile, the
Christmas present of a gelding operation **rekindling**
his enthusiasm.' *Cut* is racing's way of saying 'cas-
trate' but it is a word which has plenty of stamina to
mean other things. 'He really needs *a lot of cut*' is
not a reference to large testes but means the horse
is most *effective* in very soft conditions (where his
hooves *cut* a deep print in the turf, or what is left
of it). The phrase to *have a cut at* refers to the manner
of jumping, as in: 'He never really *had a cut at*
his fences today. Something might be **amiss**.' This
means the horse refused to *stand off* and jump boldly,
preferring to **fiddle** everything. 'The race may well
cut up' means it is unlikely many entries will stand
their ground, so that there will be few runners, or at
least few of any quality. If a horse comes **fast and
late**, he will probably *cut down* his opponents. *Mow*
and *scythe* are more roisterous alternatives in this last
situation.

Cute: Means, in professional racing anyway, battle-
hardened or clever. It can be used as a compliment to

experienced campaigners: 'There will be *more to come* from Magot de Grugy now he has an official mark, but he may still find a few of these *seasoned* handicappers *too cute*.' But perhaps more commonly the word *cute* suggests that once a horse has a *few miles on the clock* he learns not to respond so promptly to his jockey's *urgings*. This account from A. P. McCoy about a **difficult ride** is typical: 'He's hard work as he's got *a bit cute*. He never *picked up* the bridle and I hardly thought I had any chance in the straight, as all he wanted to do was **look after** himself.' It is also typical that McCoy won the race he was talking about here.

Cut each other's throats: When a number of frontrunners in the field *take each other on* at the risk of *setting the race up* for the **hold-up horses**, this inordinately brutal metaphor always comes in handy: 'Mrs Wallensky and That's an Idea *cut each other's throats* at Thurles last time.'

D

Dangerous: A staple term in race-reading shorthand, always used in the negative, as in 'short-lived effort 4f out, never *dangerous* after'. Whereas the adjective *dangerous* is always used after the race for a horse who never *got into it*, the noun *danger* is used beforehand in tipping columns for animals that will give the selection *most to do*: 'Tamarinbleu is the **nap** but Essex *rates* the *obvious danger*.' When we saw a reference in the race-reading of *Paris Turf* to a horse finishing a *platonique* fifth we expected him to be a **thinker**, but in fact this is the French equivalent to 'never *dangerous*'.

Dark horse: One of a number of expressions that presumably emanated from racing circles but that now have a wide currency in other walks of life. Plain-looking men who start going out with someone half their age are more likely to be described as *dark horses* than thoroughbreds who are difficult to *assess*: these would rather be described as *unexposed*, or *good things* if you are *in the know*.

Daylight: 'He was afforded *plenty* of *daylight* from Stall 1.' This is good news for a frontrunner in a sprint; a disaster for a horse who is a *bit keen* in a slowly run middle-distance race and needs *cover*. Jumpers can also be said to give an obstacle *daylight*, or to need *daylight* in order to *sight* their fences properly.

Dead: Race-reading is emphatically unsentimental when reporting the fact that a horse has had to be *put down*: 'Held up, progress 5 out, fell 3rd last, *dead*.' But elsewhere in the language of racing a generous quota of euphemisms to express this (see *ill-fated*, for example) frees the adjective for metaphorical purposes. So, without fear of offending any sensibilities, you may during a race speak of *dead* horses to refer to runners who are definitely *beat*. *Dead ground*, though better than *tacky* going, has no *spring* in it. *Dead wood* (or even *meat*) is a common enough cliché, but seems a particular favourite in race reports when the majority of runners were no-hopers: 'A typical mares-only contest with *plenty* of *dead wood* behind the *classy* *principals*.'

Defection: If horses do not *stand their ground* at an early acceptance stage for a big race, this is the obligatory idea: 'One Knight was among the *defectors* at the five-day stage.' Even if a horse is pulled out after being declared, the term may yet be used: 'The race was devalued by the overnight *defection* of Moscow

Flyer, who had *scoped* slightly *dirty*.' Given the incidence of Soviet *defections* (often overnight too), that of Moscow Flyer seems particularly apposite here. Elsewhere, the term would seem to be broadly synonymous with *withdrawal*, except that it perhaps lets slip a sense of disappointment or even betrayal: 'With the *defection* of Yeats, the Ballydoyle stable's hopes will be *carried* by Meath.'

Deposit: A nicely sardonic verb to describe the *unseating* of a rider: 'Algan won the 1994 *renewal* of the King George after Barton Bank had *deposited* Adrian Maguire at the last.' This is less critical of the horse than *fire out*, and less critical of the jockey than *jump off*. We have heard a similarly wry way of putting it in live commentary: 'And Dead-Eyed Dick has *decanted* Polly Gundry at the fourth last.'

Desperate: Applied primarily to ground, always meaning *desperately* bad: 'I've never seen such *desperate* ground at Chester. It was like going *through treacle*'. Also appropriate when describing a very close finish involving tired horses: 'In a *desperate affair*, Nomadic Way just got up *in the dying strides*.'

Destroyed: An alternative way of saying *put down*. Often takes *humanely*, in what looks like an oxymoron but is, for most racing people, a tautology: 'The one *sad postscript* to the race was that French Ballerina injured herself exiting the stalls and had to be *humanely destroyed*.' Sometimes the death of a horse will be remarked upon with a mixture of sentimentality and stiff upper lip: 'It at least gives me some solace that he was *killed in action* doing what he loved.'

Dick Francis novel: Journalists who refer to a mysterious incident or potential skulduggery will often feed Dick Francis with a plotline for next year's book: 'In an unfolding tale of intrigue that would *grace* a *Dick Francis novel*, the search is on for a missing racehorse removed before his intended race at Wolverhampton.'

Difference of opinion: Because it is unusual for the big firms of bookmakers to be dramatically out of line in ante-post markets, this kind of discrepancy can be noteworthy: 'Immediately after the Triumph there was a *difference of opinion*, with Ladbrokes going 12/1 Kribensis for the Champion whereas Coral were more impressed and offered only 10s.' On the racecourse the phrase is used in two instances. Sometimes the jockeys' view about the location of the best ground is not unanimous: 'A *difference of opinion* here as Michael Roberts elects to take the far rail.' And sometimes when a jockey **asks** for a *big one* his horse – often understandably – does not agree that the option is there: 'A *difference of opinion* as Strands Of Gold most emphatically *puts down* on Scu.'

Different horse: It is amazing how often horses are completely transformed by just one little thing, whether in actual fact or in their trainers' imaginations: 'Magical Wit is a *different filly* since we put the eyeshield on'; 'I promise you he'll be a *different horse* over a longer *trip*.'

Difficult ride: Although this phrase can cover a multitude of sins such as a tendency to **hang**, we may want to decode it roughly as follows: 'The horse is an idle sod who **dogs** it after a **yard** and the jockey will have to be **at it** from *pillar to post*.'

Dip: While many racecourses are undulating, there seems to be only one course that has *the dip*: the Rowley Mile at Newmarket. If you are being polite

about a horse who is running badly, you can talk of a
dip in form, but never of an abject collapse.

Dirty: 'Forget his last run as he came back with a
dirty nose.' The adjective tends to be used of noses
and throats rather than, as in other sports, to indicate
foul play (the *Dirty Derby* of 1844 won by a four-
year-old is the exception that proves the rule). These
days vets inspect a horse's trachea with an endoscope,
hence the very common formulations *scope clean* and
scope dirty: 'He *scoped dirty* this morning so we've
had to **scratch** him.'

Disappoint: A key word twice over in racing.
Whereas, more often than not, jockeys are asked to
settle or **cover** *up* their mounts, at times the act of
restraint can be catastrophic: 'I think I *disappointed*
him by taking a **pull** at the 2 pole.' You see statements
of this kind especially when somebody is making an
excuse for *going too soon*: 'Lustral du Seuil went to
the front two out, sooner than he intended, but his
jockey didn't want to *disappoint* him.' More pointedly, *disappoint* is also the universal term when a
well-fancied horse runs shockingly badly. 'He *disappointed* when he was well backed last time at
Beverley' means 'I'll never back that **nag** again – *it*
ran so badly *it* would have finished last if *it* had
joined in halfway through.'

Distress signals: These are *sent out* when a horse
comes off the bridle and the commentator can see
the jockey **scrubbing along**. The compression
required in live race-calling means it is usually the
horse that is said to send out the *signals* rather than
the jockey: 'Joanna has *turned the screw* and there's
several behind in trouble – Sudden Flight is sending
out *distress signals.*' If a horse is *distressed* (officialese
when a poor run is investigated), he will not necessar-

ily have been given the full *treatment* as more likely
something was *amiss*: 'The jockey *reported* that the
gelding swallowed his tongue and finished *distressed*.'

Dive: Jumpers, particularly hurdlers, can *dive* at an
obstacle – often with disastrous results. Meanwhile,
bookies may need to take evasive action, particularly
in ante-post markets, if new *information* comes to
light: 'Bookmakers *dived for cover*, with Coral *sticking
their neck out* in offering the winner at 14/1 from
25/1.' Sometimes the fire they are under sounds fairly
terrifying: 'We *dodged a bullet* as we were lowest price
at 7/1 on Mister McGoldrick.'

Do: 'He can't *do* lighter than 8 stone 5 nowadays';
'He's in the sauna trying to *do* 10-2.' This seems to
be the obligatory verb to convey the minimum weight
at which jockeys can ride. In their vernacular they
will also complain about being *done on the line* if
they get *touched off*. The same little verb serves to
describe all the many responsibilities of a stable lad
looking after a horse: 'Rodney *does* Quest for Fame
at home.' As for the horses themselves, to *do* is to
eat: a *good doer* puts on *condition* quickly whereas
a *bad doer* is a horse with a poor appetite. The word is
also used by punters after they have *smashed into* a
loser – 'I've *done* a *monkey* on that favourite' – or,
more sedately, when they are telling somebody else
what they are *on* in a race: 'I've *done* Tysou in this one
each way with a small *saver* on the Williams *beast*.'

Do enough: The phrase, not always especially pejorative, for a horse who *keeps something for himself*.
He is likely to win only in *workmanlike* fashion and
not to *sparkle* on the gallops: 'He only ever *does
enough* when he gets in front, but that's just him';
'He's a bit lazy and only *does enough* at home.'

Dodgepot: A portmanteau of 'dodgy' and 'hotpot', this is punters' slang for a *talking horse* you should avoid at all costs for betting purposes: 'Vodkatini rarely *consents to start* and must be the biggest *dodgepot* in racing.' Probably the mixing of drinks in the horse's name should have been an omen in this case.

Dog it: *Weighing-room* slang for a horse *downing tools*, if that isn't demotic enough: 'When they *quickened up* in front of me, he *dogged it* – just *dropped out* like he'd been *shot*.' Curious in that so many racing people own loyal and genuine dogs as pets.

Doll off: The obligatory verb in racing for any action by the racecourse staff to cordon off a fence if there has been an *incident* on the first circuit, or else to block off a particular part of the course (usually with a temporary rail tape which will blow away after five seconds). *Dolling off* seems to lead to a disproportionately large number of *farcical incidents*, and therefore *void* races, because of jockeys taking the wrong course.

Dominate: 'The Lord is at his best when he can *dominate*, but being drawn 11 isn't ideal.' The verb means 'run from the front' here, whereas, however dominant over his field a *hold-up horse* can prove to be, you would never speak of a victory from *off the pace* in this way. Jockeys who allow a *confirmed* frontrunner to *steal* a lead are sometimes criticised for allowing him to *dominate*.

Donkey work: This phrase has its predictable place in the four-legged scheme of things: 'With nothing else in the field prepared to set even a *respectable* gallop, Rooster Booster was obliged to do his own *donkey work*.' It pays tribute to the accepted wisdom – somewhat undermined by the preferred tactics of Martin

Pipe and his many imitators – that winning from the front is doing it the *hard way*.

Doss: A more colloquial alternative to *idle*: 'Macs Joy tends to *doss in front* yet still had an easy three lengths in hand at the line.' There are other racy ways of putting it: 'Dancing Bay tends not to *do a tap* in front'; 'Attitude Adjuster doesn't *do a stitch* for the whip'; 'Day Flight *has a kip* once he is in the *van*.'

Double handful: This is what a jockey *has* coming round the home turn if his mount is going strongly on the bridle. Never just a 'handful' (unless the jockey suddenly has the misfortune to *call a cab*), so that it can be described as the *proverbial double handful*. *Double wraps* is a more American-style version.

Doughty: This rather archaic word is still pertinent in racing circles to describe the important quality of *toughness*: 'Hardy Eustace will defend his title *doughtily*.' Here is another Irish trainer using an adjective from the same drawer: 'My one worry is that he's only five and that he might not be quite *hardy* enough just yet.' You will also see references, especially in previews of **bumpers**, to *stoutly bred sorts* and the odd deliberately incongruous reference to a *sprightly* eleven-year-old.

Down tools: Horses who are *cute* enough to *drop the bit* and *keep something for themselves* can be said to *down tools*. They therefore have to be *kept up* to their *work*, as in this salutary example: 'Pridwell had every excuse to *down tools* but got an exceptional ride from the champion jockey.' The outcome here looks as if it might have called for a shop-stewards' enquiry.

Draw advantage: The *trend fiends* who pay close attention to the *draw* are ignored when their findings do not correspond with a tipster's instincts: 'The *draw boys* will be out in force to get the *jolly*, who is *berthed* in stall 13, but if he is as good as I think he is, he will make light of his poor *stalls position* and win easily.' Nevertheless, the *effect* of the *draw advantage* is an excuse available to trainers whenever they are running out of others.

Drift: The most common word for what happens to the price of a horse who is *friendless* in the market: 'Sri Pekan has been *drifting* on the *exchanges* all morning.' Note that price expansion seems to be a less dramatic phenomenon than price contraction in racing markets (see *slash*).

Drive: Means to exert pressure in a measure somewhere between *hands and heels* and *rousting up*. In commentary horses can come under *strong driving*; in race-reading *driven out* is a very common way of saying that a winner just had to be *kept up* to his *work* to score. When a jockey starts *getting serious* he sits lower in the saddle, prompting observations such as: 'As they came back to him over the last, Geraghty was forced to adopt the *drive position*.'

Drop his hands: In other words, to stop *riding out* a mount: 'Fallon *dropped his hands* and *got done* on the line.' Almost without exception this expression is used when the jockey has also dropped a clanger by relaxing too soon and, in the argot of the Jockey Club Rule 151 (ii), has failed to get the *best possible placing* for his horse. You would never commentate on a *facile* win by saying: 'He's winning this so easily that Keiren's *dropped his hands*.' *Won hands down*, the obvious usage in these circumstances, is so common in other fields that you would instead tend to select one of the other available terms for a rider who has *eased up* (see *handbrake*).

Drop out: This is nothing to do with having anti-social tendencies, but almost everything to do with having tactical awareness: 'Paul Carberry *dropped him out* early and then **produced** him with a devastating late run.' Meanwhile, trainers regularly instruct jockeys to *drop* their horse *in*. *Dropping in* is not fundamentally opposed to *dropping out*, but the technical distinction is that in the first case the jockey gets his mount **covered** *up* among other horses, while in the second he prefers to sit *right out the back*. We can still conceive of there being 'dropouts' in racing, but only in the sense that horses *drop out of contention*, which they usually do quite convincingly: 'Regal Party ran *very free* giving chase to the leader in the early stages until *dropping right away*.'

Dual-purpose: Describes a horse that can run effectively in two or more types of race. For example, the phrase can be used for a horse switching from the *all-weather* to turf, or from larger obstacles to hurdles. But it applies most commonly to animals who can adapt to both *codes* (and so also to the activities of *dual-purpose trainers*). The following case history is fairly typical: 'We bought him as a *dual-purpose horse* and will have him *castrated* in March, and give him a break then. We'll have some *fun* with him on the *flat* first, but I'm really looking forward to *sending* him *hurdling* at the end of next year.' *Dual-purpose* horses, or animals who switch between **birch** and *timber*, can be described as having a *mix-and-match campaign*. Perhaps they are entitled to become confused: 'Back over the smaller obstacles he'll think he's in a *meadow*.' However single-minded, stallions are *dual-purpose* if they sire both flat horses and jumpers.

Duck: Apt if connections try to avoid taking each other on, but used likewise when bookmakers take no chances with liabilities on one horse: 'We are happy

to be top price and there is no point in *ducking* him.'
Flat horses *duck in* when they refuse to go past other
runners in a finish; jump horses *duck out* when they
avoid jumping a fence by going the wrong side of the
wings.

Dulux: 'One Cool Cat looked like someone had
poured *Dulux* down his legs.' A horse who is *awash
with sweat* might be described thus, as the white for-
mation of the perspiration can look like paint. There
is probably also a verbal trigger at work in the idea of
a 'gloss finish'.

Dwelt: Invariably the word for horses who begin
races slowly, particularly out of starting stalls, so that
many pieces of race-reading in summer months begin
with: *'Dwelt start . . .'*

E

Each-way chance: 'On his best form, you'd have to
give him an *each-way chance*.' This often means, as
here, 'not at all **expected**' or 'Don't put your mortgage
on the **nag** whatever you do.' The *chance* sometimes
becomes a *squeak*, whereas *solid each-way claims* are
more substantial. Connections who say they are betting only *each way* may be more than *covering* themselves on another horse, and tend to be described as
hopeful rather than *confident*.

Earn his fee: 'Tony McCoy had to *earn his fee* on the
inexperienced Shower Of Hail.' This means that A.P.
will have been *hard at work* on the horse from a very
long way out and will certainly not have had time to
work out his **percentage**. A jump jockey's race fee in

Britain is currently £107.92. If he takes one unplaced
spare at an evening meeting at Kelso, he probably has
enough left, after payments to his *agent*, his *valet* and
sundry filling stations, to cover a lager top and a packet
of pork scratchings. But he's not even allowed those.

Ears pricked: Received wisdom is that these are the
sure sign of an alert and willing horse. Yet if a runner
is five lengths clear of a pursuer with equally erect
lobes, the commentator will only remark upon the
leader: 'And so Fundamentalist comes home, *ears
pricked* . . .' The same observation can also have
entirely the opposite implication if the horse is thought
to be distracted by the noise of the crowd or not to be
concentrating on the job in hand: 'Despite *pricking his
ears* and *idling*, Contraband came clear on the run-in.'

Eat the turf: Should a horse *peck* very badly on landing, but get away with the mistake, this is the formula: 'Clan Royal *ate the turf* at Becher's first time
round but made up the ground well.' *Kissed the turf* is
a more nuanced way of putting it, while to say that a
horse *nosed on landing* or was *down on his **nose*** is less
ironically couched.

Effing: Trainers are notorious for their use of the
f-word, particularly when Jim Lewis is singing.
Although not as accepted as *bollocking* and *knackered*, the bowdlerised form does turn up in racing
journalism, most famously in Fred Winter's often-
quoted dictum: 'There are three tracks in Britain
starting with F: Folkestone, Fakenham and *effing*
Plumpton.' Perhaps John Francome had Winter's
remark in his subconscious when he was asked on
The Morning Line which three British racecourses had
parts of the body embedded in their names: 'I didn't
know Scunthorpe had a racecourse.' For the record,
the answer is *Chest*er, *Liver*pool and Yar*mouth*.

Egg-and-spoon race: 'The Irish are not frightened
to take anything on in the very best novice hurdle
races in their *Racing Calendar*, whereas British winners of the Supreme have tended to potter about in
egg-and-spoon races before being unleashed on the big
stage'. The implication is of a primary-school jaunt,
with no-hopers falling about, as opposed to the *rough
and tumble* of competitive racing. Such contests never
take much winning. We have seen a similar analogy
after objections to a jockey's alleged rough-house
tactics in a big race: 'This is the Cheltenham Gold
Cup not an *effing gymkhana*.'

Embryo chaser: A horse for whom *anything* over
hurdles will be a *bonus*, as connections believe they
have a *big future* over the larger obstacles: 'Darkness
won't have the speed to go with *pacy* flat *types* over
two miles, but he's an *embryo chaser* for next year if
ever I saw one.' Trainers usually can't wait to see
their *embryo chasers* *pop* a *fence*.

Empty: Features in one of those frequent metaphors
comparing horses to cars: 'His *tank* just *emptied* at
the two furlong marker'; 'He was *running on empty*
from some way out'; 'He *emptied* very quickly from
the last.' Of these three slightly different ways of
putting it, the last is the most common, and jockeys
can even complain about how a horse *empties on*
them.

End-to-end: You don't find 'end-to-end stuff' in
racing as you do in football, but you can get an *end-
to-end gallop*. The purists will be happy because such
a *truly run* race tends to be a better spectacle than a
messy, *tactical* affair, while the *form students* will be
pleased because the even gallop should provide an
uncomplicated indication of the runners' ability.

Engine: It is naturally exciting to see and sense a horse that is going *at full throttle* or *firing on all cylinders*. However, there is more to jump racing than stamina in the form of power under the bonnet, as these more reflective examples suggest: 'Rule Supreme has such a tremendous *engine* but jumping is just not his strength'; 'Doubts remain over Inglis Drever's jumping and inclination to *run in **snatches*** but his three-length defeat of Baracouda at Cheltenham emphasises that he has a strong *engine.*'

Enjoy: The standard mantra of connections who keep an *old* soldier in training long past his normal *sell-by date* is more or less as follows: 'The owners *love* him *to death* and the minute he tells us he's *not enjoying it* he'll be retired.' During a race it is usually those horses who are ***bowling along*** who are said to be *enjoying themselves* or, if they are well clear, *really enjoying themselves*.

Enterprising: Likely to describe any ride in which a combination *slips the field*. Riding a *waiting* race would never be *enterprising* but would invite such terms as *patient, nerveless* or *well-judged*.

Entitled: What trainers tend to say when they are convincing themselves they should run because a *strict interpretation* of the form book tells them they should win: 'Hardy Eustace is *entitled* to beat Solerina and so he'll take his chance.' Also employed in the same specific way when reporting on the outcome of a race: 'Lady Zephyr was *entitled* to win this contest, as she did, on official figures.' However, if you read form guides for a living you might be forgiven for developing the impression that horses can be *entitled* to just about anything: 'After Me Boys is *entitled* to need the run'; 'Moldavia is *entitled* to find improvement for her debut effort.'

Equine: This term will naturally occur in a medical context with talk of *equine surgeons* or *equine physiotherapy*. But the Latinism usually brings a touch of style when discussion moves on to celebrating *equine legends* or horses that have been admitted to the *equine pantheon*. The stylistic effect is a bit more difficult to gauge in this recent observation on the activities of the Godolphin operation in Dubai: 'The men who supervise this array of *equine galacticos* are calculatingly conservative in their predictions.'

Every inch: 'Stormez will *relish every inch* of the *extended* 3m 2f'; 'Over The Creek looks *every inch* the *embryo chaser*': two common situations where the tape measure is brought out to emphasise the length of a stayer's required ***trip*** or the ***scope*** of a horse.

Exes: Professional racing is a tight little circuit where ex-spouses or lovers will bump into each other, but if you hear this expression in the ring it will be somebody talking about 6/1 in backslang. Other common examples of this bookmaking argot include *rouf, enin* and *net*.

Expected: With 'to win' understood, describes the pregnant anticipation of a stable who believe they are onto a *good thing*: 'She was *expected* today so it's gratifying to see her win so well.'

Expensive to follow: A more aloof way of saying that a horse has not been running to its best form: 'Rooster Booster retains ***plenty*** of *dash*, but has been *expensive to follow* since winning two years ago and may again *flatter to deceive.*' Probably the followers of this particular horse were to some extent indulging the general fondness for a grey.

Exposed: Because very few horses are *classy* enough never to run in handicaps, the terms *unexposed* and *exposed* usually stand in racing parlance for 'good' and 'bad'. Possibly derived from whist, the terms recognise the fact that trainers try to keep a *good thing* secret and even then will try not to show their full hand until they are ready. Any horse who is *unexposed* in this way therefore has the potential to keep *improving*. While there is no reason to believe that *exposed* horses cannot *reproduce* their form, experience tells racegoers that horses tend to be on the *upgrade* or the *downgrade* with little in between, and therefore *exposed* tends to mean 'not good enough': 'Dear Deal is *exposed* as a *plodder*, but he jumps well and could sneak into the *frame*.'

Express train: By now a dated comparison, usually for a horse coming very late *on the* **scene**. Perhaps this is why jockeys are sometimes said to be *stoking the coals*. Since the horse in question has come with a *rattling* run which is sadly far too late, a modernised version alluding to the punctuality of Virgin Trains would be apposite, but we have not yet heard it attempted by a racecourse commentator.

Extended: Ubiquitous term meaning 'a tad further' than the *distance* measured in round figures. So, we meet specifications like 'over an *extended* six furlongs . . .' or 'over an *extended* three miles . . .' While **facile** winners can also be said to land the spoils *unextended*, hard-pressed winners would not be referred to as 'extended', although you are allowed to observe that the winner had to *stretch out*.

Eye in: A concept borrowed from cricket to suggest that jumping, on the schooling ground or in the heat of a race, gets easier once you have had some **match** *practice*: 'We **popped** Sweet Kiln over a hurdle this morning to *get her eye in* and she *winged* it.' When talking about a *barrier **trial*** or a racetrack gallop, the Australians can also compare the workout to a light net: 'It's full steam ahead to Brisbane for unbeaten sprinter Takeover Target after emerging unscathed from a *hit out* at Queanbeyan.'

F

Face: A punter well known to the layers: 'A *face* came in for the horse at the opening show of 5/2 and that price wasn't seen again.' Often used in the plural as a collective term for those *in the know*: 'The *faces* seem to be backing this Kerry Lads.'

Facile: Racing is one of the few worlds where this word still retains its Latinate meaning of *easy* over and above the modern meaning of 'superficial'. Indeed, a *facile* victory is perhaps the race-reader's most superlative version of an 'easy win'. They have a variety of other pithy terms for a bloodless success, not always easy to list in order of ease: *pushed out, not extended, impressive, hard-held* are the adjectives; *cosily, cheekily, cleverly, readily, easily, very easily* the adverbs. The ***weighing-room*** vernacular for a *facile* win is *pissed up* or *pissed it*: 'Kieren got off and said she absolutely *pissed up.*' Connections will often then recreate the ***manner*** of victory in the *owners' and trainers' bar*.

Facilities: Racing is increasingly being marketed as a *great day out* with fun for all the family and to that end racecourses emphasise the *facilities* on offer. We remember an announcement repeated at frosty Kempton Park many years back, when the reality perhaps had not caught up with the vocabulary: 'Racing has been abandoned. However, you do have full use of the *facilities*.' The Gents' toilets were unlocked.

Faller: The noun prospers in racing commentary such that it is as plausible to say 'Monsieur Le Cure was the *faller* there' as 'Monsieur Le Cure fell at that one.' Whereas you are unlikely to catch someone saying after an evening on the town 'I was a faller in the street last night.'

Fall out of the stalls: 'Form students should ignore Airwave's run as she *fell out of the stalls* and *gave up all chance* there.' A way of indicating that the horse was *slowly into its stride* at the start or *missed the* **break**, in flat-race terminology. Usually explains why a horse was beaten. For the opposite, you can say *fly the gate* or, more surprisingly, **jump off**.

Fancy: Correspondents writing copy that genuinely tries to give punters a view on all the horses in the race will tend to eschew grand subjective statements about their own *selection*. Instead, you will see comments such as these: 'Galveston is *fancied* to win here'; 'Queen Astrid *gets the vote* to score.' But the noun *fancy* has a pejorative tinge in racing. Used of horses, it is a near synonym for **talking** in the racing sense: 'The **tough** little gelding has achieved more than his more *fancy* rivals.' Used of prices offered by layers in the ring or on the exchanges, it suggests overgenerosity on their part: 'The five-year-old was matched at *fancy* prices throughout the day.'

Farm: 'Philip Hobbs has now *farmed* this race three times in four years.' When a trainer turns a particular race into something of a **benefit**, this is definitely the verb to use, although it can apply to any shrewd placing of a horse: 'Connections are understandably drooling at the prospect of Mel In Blue switching to the larger obstacles next season, but in the meantime they are *farming* minor events over *timber*.' Especially appropriate for the many yards located on working or converted farms.

Fast and late: Just as bowlers aspire to achieve *fast and late* swing, so jockeys on **hold-up horses** dream of *arriving* or *swooping* in this way. Such a late entrance *on the* **scene**, provided you have not left yourself *too much to do*, all but guarantees victory, so *late* in effect means 'timely' here: 'At Epsom only a length separated the first eight home as Caribbean Coral *arrived fast and late*.'

Favourite backers: '*Favourite backers* had their hopes temporarily raised when 16/1 shot River Marshal *fluffed his lines* at the second last.' In racing prose, and especially round-ups of the previous day's meetings, *favourite backers* are mentioned as a kind of index to the number of upsets. This is such a useful device for giving continuity to their reports that correspondents momentarily overlook the fact that it is unusual for even the most unimaginative of punters to back favourites all day. A corollary is that the *anxious moments* which *favourite backers* may or may not have is a clue to the margin of the victory: 'Those who had sent the John Dunlop colt off at 8/11 never had an *anxious moment*.'

Favouritism: Racing inflects this term in its own way, emptying it of its customary moral charge, for while people would not want to be accused of it, horses may with impunity *vie for favouritism* before a race and, if all goes well, *justify* it after: 'Berenson *justified favouritism* in his maiden at the Curragh by a length and a half from another newcomer Sanserif.'

Featherweight: Used either of horses who may be a *blot* on the handicap or, more rarely, of jockeys who can *do* light weights: 'The winner will be a *featherweight* in the Lincoln, even with a penalty'; '*Featherweight* Richard Fox is *up*.' 'Paper', 'bantam' or 'fly' weights never seem to be required in racing.

Feel: 'David Casey rode him last time, hopped off and said "My God he *gave me* a tremendous *feel*".' When jockeys *get* or are *given a feel* it is, perhaps disappointingly, merely in response to the way a horse has **travelled** in a race or on the gallops: 'It was a nice easy work and Grand Central gave me a *nice feel*.' Very often a jockey will report that something is **amiss** by comparing the *feel* a horse has given him previously: 'He never gave me the *same feel* as at Newbury last time and I was never happy.'

Feel the effects: When a horse runs without **zest** after a hard race or a busy season (or both), this is the set phrase: 'Turned out quickly after his win to escape a penalty, he looked *as if* he was *feeling the effects* of his arduous campaign.'

Feel the pinch: 'Dungarvan's Choice was beginning to *feel the pinch* when getting the last on the far side *all wrong* and paying the penalty.' *Pinch* means 'pace' here, and may also allude to the **assistance** the jockey will be giving (**hands and heels** at the very least) in these circumstances.

Feet: *Up on their feet* or *up on their feet all right* is the standard way for a commentator to let us know that *both horse and jockey* have emerged from a fall unscathed. It seems to matter little that in both cases they can be seriously injured even if they do regain their *feet*. When jockeys are said to *resume the perpendicular*, the comically posh, circumlocutory tone adds an extra guarantee that we need not worry about any injury. It is rare to hear references to horses' *feet*, in stark contrast to the number of times you will find trainers talking about one of their *legs*, although note the phrase relating to poor jumpers: 'Pizarro would be a top-class chaser if only he could *pick his feet up.*'

Fence: Trainers, and sometimes journalists too, seem to think in schematic terms when they look forward to a horse coming back from a layoff, being **schooled** or taking on the bigger obstacles for the first time. *Crossing* one *fence* seems to be representative: 'Strong Flow jumped *a fence* for the first time in more than a year yesterday'; 'Gallery God has taken well to hurdling and connections feel he will *jump a fence* in time.' Rhythmical jumpers can be praised for jumping from *fence to fence*, as in this example: 'Grey Abbey got an *uncontested* lead and jumped beautifully from *fence to fence.*' Quite how else Grey Abbey was supposed to have jumped is unclear.

Ferrari: 'It was a pleasure to ride Moscow Flyer knowing there was nothing capable of beating him. It was like sitting in a *Ferrari* when no one else has one'; 'Dancing Brave is like the feeling you get when you drive a good car: power and acceleration. This horse is a *Porsche.*' Whereas the riders of very *classy* animals readily reach for comparisons to cars, the riders of less successful horses never seem to compare their mounts to, say, a clapped-out Fiat 126.

Festival: The *Festival* is the March meeting at Cheltenham (the town has also borrowed the title for some minor literary convention). Most racecourses in Ireland also call their main meeting of the year a *Festival*: one of the most famous is at Galway, where perhaps strangely you only get a *Plate* for winning the feature race. The Australian for *Festival* is

Carnival, and there is certainly this kind of atmosphere on Melbourne Cup day, which is a public holiday in Victoria. Argentina takes no bank holidays for racing, but note that 2 August is the National Day of the Salaried Employee in Racehorse Administration.

Fiddle: Although there can be a hint of scepticism in live commentary – 'Kildimo *fiddled* that one' – the ability of a chaser to *fiddle*, in other words to shorten his stride without *putting down*, and so negotiate the obstacle safely, if not always gracefully, is an important one: 'The great thing about him is that, as well as the spectacular leaps from *outside the **wings***, he can *fiddle* them if he has to.' We have also seen the verb used, perhaps with slight connotations of Rome burning or more possibly with echoes of an Irish ceilidh at heart, when a trainer promises he will be running a horse regularly without having a specific target: 'He **handles** soft ground so we'll just *fiddle away* with him for the time being.'

Field: In commentary, can mean all the horses – 'As the *field* turn out into the **country** . . .' ; 'And the *field* is splitting into two groups . . .' – or just those horses in the main **pack**: 'Benbyas has *slipped* his *field*'; 'Champleve is coming back to his *field*.' In betting, only the majority of the runners is being referred to, so that *the field* can be a synonym for *bar*: 'They go 14/1 *the field*.' Meanwhile tipsters or punters can speak of the two or three runners they have selected *against the field*.

Find: Invariably, when horses *come off* the bridle – so often the crucial moment in the race – they are **asked** to *find* something by their jockeys. It is much more usual to comment on those who *find* **nothing** or *little* than those who *find* **plenty**. Not least because of the colloquial opportunities such as 'I'm afraid Harchibald doesn't *find ten bob* off the bridle' and 'Barbilyrifle *finds blankety-blank* off the bit.'

Fire: If you hear of a horse having been *fired*, it is not P45 time but a case of a painful operation to strengthen the tendons in his legs. Jockeys are *fired from the saddle* in circumstances where they cannot be blamed for being **unseated**. *Firing* (often with *on all cylinders* added) can also be used to describe the good or bad form of a stable: 'Power Elite represents Noel Meade, whose team has not been *firing* since Christmas.' The well-being of an animal can be verified with an alliterative phrase: 'He's swum and cantered and jumped and he's as *fit as fire.'*

First Lady: The Queen Mother used to be the *First Lady* of National Hunt racing, but the title can yet be conferred on mares who dominate a division. For example, Dawn Run in her time and now Solerina are two horses to have been described as the *First Lady* of Irish jumping. Whereas Charmian Hill, Dawn Run's owner, was the *Galloping Granny*.

Fizzy: An adjective to describe horses who are a *bit keen*, especially if they are *on their toes* in the *preliminaries*. Handlers like to see their horses *sparkle*, but not excessively so: 'We ran Ballybough Rasher over hurdles to take the *fizz* out of him before a chasing campaign.' But note that this *prep race* would not be designed to take the *edge* off the horse. Synonyms for *fizzy* are *buzzy* (or *buzzed up*) and *revvy* (or *revved up*).

Flat spot: Horses who *run in snatches* experience these – the moments when the jockey *presses the button* and gets no *immediate response*. Used particularly when the horse in question has a history of not getting stuck in a *flat spot* for the entire race. Can even take shape as a verb: 'Inglis Drever *flat-spotted* a couple

of times but was back **hard on the steel** by the last.' If
you are *flat out* it is not always a bad thing, especially
if you have *flattened out* like a *greyhound*. However, if a
jockey reports his mount to have *run*, or to *be*, a *bit flat*,
he suspects something is slightly **amiss**.

Flatten: What horses can do to *flights* of hurdles of
traditional timber construction (but not French hurdles now installed at several courses). There is a more
flamboyant way of putting it: 'French Holly has *kicked*
that flight *out of the ground.'* This frequently happens
later in races and the jockeys not involved in the finish seem hypnotically drawn to steering their mounts
through the gap in the hurdle, even if they get in each
others' way or have to change course in the process.

Flat to the boards: 'Good Citizen is now *flat to the
boards* and making *no impression.'* One of the horse-
as-car metaphors recurrent especially in commentary
(see **empty**).

Flip-flop: What market leaders do when there is a
dispute over **favouritism** and first one and then the
other is the shorter price: 'We've got *flip-flopping*
favourites here but it looks like Turbo will eventually
be *sent off* the **jolly.'***

Fluency: A common measure of jumping ability,
especially when you want to emphasise quick, rhythmical jumping – though the word is actually used
most often to comment rather mildly on poor jumping: 'Seagram was *none too fluent* at that one'; 'La
Landiere was not jumping with her *usual fluency.'***

Fluff his lines: 'Lord Sam, who *fluffed his lines* in the
Charlie Hall at Wetherby, looks to make amends at
Newbury.' This cliché is usually reserved for jumping
errors but can be seen on the flat if a well-fancied

favourite disappoints: 'Exceed And Excel *fluffed his lines* in Thursday's big race and was promptly retired.' In both circumstances the horses could also have *blotted their copybooks*.

Fly a kite: Rare but very graphic metaphor for the action of a jockey with the proverbial ***double handful***, pulling hard on either side of his reins to keep his mount restrained, with the result that the horse's head swings from side to side as he ***pulls*** *for* it: 'Who can forget Niall Madden *flying a kite* with the ***illfated*** Golden Cygnet, so well were they ***travelling*** at the second last.' The image is used to point out that a horse is going exceptionally well in a race; it would be impolite to use it when a young apprentice is being *carted* down to post by something *a bit too* ***keen***.

Flyer: When a jockey *gets a flyer* he may well have been handed an invitation to the ***Abba*** tribute band's post-racing set, but, almost as likely, he can have *slipped his field* at the start of a race. The phrase is equally attributable to the horse itself. This may be particularly appropriate when a sprinter has *exploded* from the stalls: 'Indian Ridge has *caught* a *right flyer* there from the inside draw.' But while the phrase is used on the flat, it appears most reliably in ***little*** jumps races, notably when the starter lifts the tapes to find that the race's only frontrunner is ready, while most of the rest of the field are facing in the opposite direction or are completely ***planted***: 'David Dennis was *on his toes* at the start there and *got* an *absolute flyer*. He's already 20 lengths clear of the field.' Finally, as well as *getting* a *flyer*, a horse can actually be a *Flyer*, in the sense that its owner, hopefully but often inappropriately, has tagged it with this name.

Form: *Form* is definitely the gold standard when it comes to predicting future performance. Indeed,

reference can be made to *form* which is *blue-chip*, or
has a *solid look* about it, even if it was difficult to *weigh
up* or *quantify* before hand (see *frank the form*). *Form*
students are more wary of any race that may not produce reliable *collateral form lines*: 'Not *form* to *take* at
face value, as the early pace was slow and Winston
was gifted a soft lead.' They know that some entries
in the *form book* can be more worthy of note than
others – 'Posh Stick's Cartmel win in August *reads
quite well*' – and that the *bare form* can be misleading
in all sorts of ways: 'The way it's *written in the
book* doesn't do full justice to Tamarinbleu, as he
turned what was a frighteningly competitive race into
a *procession*.'

Form book: In other sports the *form book* tends to be
metaphorical, but in racing it really exists. Even after
the demise of the blue *Sporting Chronicle* form books,
which certain trainers of the old school lined up next
to their Wisdens, there are many available sources
for a record of previous races. Most serious form
students now swear by the *Racing Post*'s remarkably
comprehensive internet site, which serves as their
virtual form book. But it is harder to throw a computer
out of the window.

Forward: While it can describe the readiness of any
horse – 'We've got See More Business much more
forward than in previous years' – it is usually reserved
for precocious two- or three-year-olds: 'Seallarain will
be our first juvenile runner at Musselburgh today and
how she gets on will give us an idea of how *forward*
the two-year-olds are.' With *squiggle horses*, only
they know when they will deign to put their *best foot
forward*.

Four faults: A Mark Johnsonism, borrowed from
show jumping, to tick off a horse for not getting *very*

high at his obstacles: 'Free Return was the one who got *four faults* at that open ditch.' We have also heard Johnson, a brilliant annotator of how horses jump their fences (perhaps because he *calls* many races *between the flags*), use another show-jumping term: 'Comply Or Die jumped that one as if it was a *puissance wall* and gave it *plenty of air.*' The concept of a *clear round* is less idiosyncratic: sometimes (compare *stand up*) it is what dodgy jumpers only need to *put in* to win.

Fractions: In countries with a tradition of independent bookmaking, *fractions* are what you get if you are a preferred client and receive odds of, say, 100/6 rather than 16/1. In those countries that value sectional timings, *fractions* are the clock figures in which horses *get* each quarter-mile: 'Mauk Four raced through *fractions* of 23.50 for the opening quarter and 47.76 for the half-mile mark, all while being *stalked* by Free Thinking.' The American obsession with *splits* may seem strange to us. But what the British and Irish gain with their wonderful variety of racecourse configurations they lose in terms of being able to compare exactly how races have *panned out* over the same distance. The uniform nature of *main tracks* in the States allows their horseplayers to take a delight in sophisticated *clocking*. Perhaps it is significant that Cole Porter compared his beloved not to a top racehorse but to 'the *time* of the Derby winner' (even if he did need a rhyme for 'sublime').

Frame: The metaphor is dying, in that fewer racecourses put the racecard numbers of placed horses in a *frame*, but it is accepted almost universally to mean 'in the first three' (or four if the bookies are accepting *each-way* bets that far). *In the money* tends to have a similar meaning, even when prize money actually extends down to sixth or seventh place. As a verb, the handicapper or race-planner can *frame* the conditions of a race to attract a certain type of runner: 'With other options around Christmas in both Britain and Ireland for top chasers, the Paddy Power is *framed* specifically for those who are not much better than useful handicappers, with a rating limit of 140.' Very occasionally, a new race is *framed* for a particular horse – Cigar and Best Mate have had races established for them in this way.

Frank: 'Lady Zephyr *franked* the form'; 'The form was *franked* when the winner **bolted** up again next time out.' This usage is so established that you can hardly see the join between the two meanings of the word *form*. *Rubber-stamp* acts as a straight substitute, while *endorse* can work the same idea: 'Kauto Star was widely expected to *endorse* his status as short-priced favourite for the Arkle.'

Freshen up: Horses can be *freshened up*, as you might expect, by a *break*, but also by a run. If they are turning into **thinkers**, they can also be *freshened up* by a *spell* in the *hunting field* or a *spin* on the *Cambridge Road Polytrack*. Racing people can talk about themselves in the same way, as in this quote from jockey Paul Hanagan: 'In retrospect the time off may have *freshened me up* for the closing months of the season.'

Freshman: The universal term for a horse of either sex yet to win a race is *maiden*, and jockeys sometimes admit to being *virgins* at a certain meeting; but the term for first-season stallions is rather prim, as if they are attending college rather than *covering* every day: '*Freshmen* sires Hawkeye, Birdstone and Ransom O'War all had their first mares *scanned* in foal recently.' That said, the term allows breeders to anticipate their sires *graduating* a year later, and may not be entirely inappropriate given the activities of the students who used to *cover* for us in our first year at college.

From: The humble preposition is privileged in racing commentary when it comes to enumerating runners in current or finishing order: 'Muse *from* Halkopous *from* Royal Derbi.' Grand prix commentators describing a procession of cars rather than horses will typically prefer 'then' as the interconnecting preposition. But the real privilege is to be able to listen to a commentator who can put together a sequence like the following: '*Next comes* Firebreak, *pursued by* Indian Haven, *next in the field* is Ikhtyar, *behind him* Gateman, *followed by* Refuse to Bend, *then comes* Checkit, *shuffled back* through the field is Tout Seul, with Desert Deer *whipping them in* at this stage.' The *shuffled back* is a master touch (see also ***pack***).

Fun horse: 'Brave Spirit may have been bought merely as a *fun horse* by Colin Tizzard, but he holds a great chance of ***collecting*** the Southern National at Fontwell today.' While a *fun horse* can occasionally transform into a ***serious*** one, the more usual translation is 'a ***nag*** producing no financial return whatsoever for the owner'. If your trainer describes your horse as such, prepare for his failing to return your phone calls, only entering the horse when another of his *fun horses* is entered at the same (undoubtedly ***gaff***) track, and drinking champagne with better-dressed connections while you have half a shandy with the *lad*.

G

Gaff track: 'He's *run up* a little sequence at the *gaffs*, but he's been *upped* into stiffer company here at

Ascot.' An unflattering term for the less glamorous provincial tracks, which rarely have meetings on Saturdays (*gaff* originally meant 'fair'). Americans who call up-country venues *leaky-roof tracks* may be surprised to learn that at some British *gaffs* there is not even a roof on the stand. However, it is a badge of faith for National Hunt enthusiasts to prefer the atmosphere here to the bigger meetings. The Bishop Auckland trainer Arthur Stephenson would choose to saddle runners at Hexham or Sedgefield during the Cheltenham Festival. Note also the nice little adaptation of the cricket expression 'flat-track bully' for a horse who likes it *all his own way*: 'Before his recent success over the reliable Wain Mountain, I always had Mouseski down as a *gaff-track bully.*'

Gallop: The fastest of a horse's *paces*, at which all races are run even if they can be won – metaphorically – at a ***canter***. *Gallop* is therefore a synonym for *pace*: 'They went a *good gallop* in this one from *pillar to post.*' A *real* (sometimes *old-fashioned*) *galloper* is a long-striding horse who can keep up a good level speed throughout a race, even if he might lack ***gears***. He is more effective on a *galloping* track (Newbury is the most cited example in England) which is flat with easy bends (and preferably *easy* going): 'The winner is nothing more than a relentless *galloper* who operates in this *testing* ground.' Outside the British Isles, *galloper* is a routine synonym for a *racehorse* of any type, perhaps because of the contrast with ***trotting*** horses: 'Struggling *gallopers* having their tenth crack at a *maiden* don't really have looks'; 'Royal Ascot's head of PR Nick Smith is keen to lure more of Australia's premier *gallopers* to the English *carnival* of racing.' In the plural, *gallops* refer to the part of a training establishment (often *all-weather* these days) where the horses work (hence *on the gallops* is a synonym for *at home*). Trainers will often advertise themselves by emphasising the excellence or variety of their *gallops*.

Game: Can be used of the *industry* as a whole, or to distinguish the summer *game* from the winter one (*code* is equally available in this context). But most frequently employed about a particular horse's specialism: 'Three mile novice chasing has always been his *game*.' As an adjective, *game* often accompanies *genuine*.

Gammy: Originally a technical if slang term, in that horses with overworked tendons tend to be puffy below the hocks. Now used of any *leg problem*, and probably more of humans than of horses.

Gears: 'He's got *gears*.' In other words, he is not *one-paced*. Particularly important in flat racing, where a *turn of foot* is essential: 'He went *through the gears* quickly and impressively, coming from last to first in a *matter of strides*.' When you read about a change of *gear* in an Australian newspaper, it is much more likely to refer to the application or removal of an *aid*: 'Deagon trainer Shaun Dwyer has also made a crucial *gear change* with Succeeding, who will carry blinkers when she resumes in the Gray-Buchanan.' Indeed, these *gear changes* are announced in advance and are a lot more detailed than in Britain and Ireland: 'CREDERE: Blinkers Off Concussion Plates (Front) First Time, Nose Roll First Time Pads (Front) Off.' With all this equipment to declare it is probably as well that Ned Kelly races in Ireland.

Gee-gee: A colloquialism far more likely to be used of Graham Goode than by him.

Gelding: *Cut* animals are the rule in jumps racing, for reasons Major Fitzgeorge-Parker outlines in his usual brisk fashion: 'Most horses understandably *fall out of love* with the ***game*** and turn *sour* when they scratch their testicles repeatedly on the tops of the fences.' Journalists tend to use the word neutrally to avoid repeating the name of a horse in successive clauses, although the way in which they regularly name the sire in these cases may rub things in: 'Korelo looked the *likely* winner but the Cadoudal gelding could ***find*** *no more* up the hill.'

Gentleman: More likely to designate a horse than a human, even in the smarter enclosures: 'Dessie, realising his fun was over, pulled up like a *gentleman.*' Stables understandably grow fond of certain animals who are *true gentlemen* or *true Christians*: 'The horse was a *gentleman* in his box and a *good doer.*' A *gentleman's gallop* is a slow one, although for many amateurs the problem is keeping horses under *restraint* rather than getting them ***stoked up***.

Genuine: 'Lord Of The River is a most ***game*** and *genuine* ***sort***, and a ***credit*** to his connections.' *Genuine* horses, whatever their ***ability***, never display ***in and out*** form or turn out to be ***difficult rides***. You are placing more of an emphasis on *class* if you say that a horse is the *genuine article*.

Get: An important little word with a whole variety of meanings depending on the accompanying preposition or adverb. Punters spend most of the day trying to *get on* their selections at attractive prices (or at any price at all in the maelstrom of the ring at Cheltenham). Then, betting on the ***lucky last***, they seek to *get out* by covering their losses for the meeting with a final large bet. If this fails they can have problems, like the *non-stayer* they may have backed, *getting home*. Horses are said to *get in* to handicaps if their official mark gives them a weight above the minimum. They are said to *get up* if they come out best in a close finish – 'And the mare's *getting up*. She's beginning to *get up*' – but this does not mean they have been on the floor. Jockeys *get off* a horse before they have even sat on it in circumstances where they elect to ride a more fancied runner in preference to another they have been *booked* for. See also *trip* and *throw* for usages that do not require a preposition.

Get in the way: What the obstacles tend to do when a none-too-clever jumper is endeavouring to clear them: 'The occasional fence *gets in the way*, but he's very *game* and a *fluent round* would take him close.'

Get on well: Just as a rider may *get a tune* out of a horse, so a jockey and his mount can seem to make friends. Perhaps our imagination, but this phrase seems to be used with particular regularity by trainers putting a *girl* up to ride: 'Lorraine *gets on well* with the horse and the gelding seems better suited by this track.'

Give away: Bookmakers apparently struggle to do this when one of the market leaders is *alarmingly* on the *drift*: 'The on-course *layers* couldn't *give away* Toulouse-Lautrec, who *weakened* from 5/2 to 5/1.' Never true, of course.

Give notice: We learn from form students, usually with the safety of hindsight, that a horse had already warned us with a previous performance of his potential *ability* over a different distance or track: 'Keltic Rock had *given notice* that he would *improve* for this longer *trip*.' We have not seen the phrase when the form suggests that a horse might consider early retirement.

Glass: 'He's made of *glass* and is very high maintenance'; 'His legs are *glass* and you have to treat him
with kid gloves.' When a trainer wants to emphasise
the fragility of a horse, this is the metaphor he will
probably reach for, if he is not already at the bar con-
soling the owners about the horse *breaking down*. It's
difficult to tell sometimes who is feeling the more
fragile: 'Creskeld has *dodgy knees* and we are *walking
on eggshells* with him.'

Glorious: The Goodwood festival meeting enjoys a
virtual monopoly on this adjective, which tends to
stick so faithfully to the noun that we once heard a
hapless punter confess to having 'a really awful
Glorious Goodwood'.

Gluey: Apart from an occasional reference to the
adhesive qualities of jump jockeys, *glue* is a term that
refers to the state of the ground: 'It was *gluey* and
they weren't kicking up any *sod*.' In other words, even
horses who prefer **cut** might have difficulty **sluicing**
through such ground. *Tacky* and *sticky* are companion terms to *gluey*, but you wouldn't mix them
together without consulting the instructions.

Go close: 'Like-A-Butterfly *should go close*.' Tipsters –
at least those that do not have premium-rate phone
lines – have a variety of ways of saying they think
a horse will win, but with enough humility or nous
to hedge their expression. The regular contenders
include: *should take all the beating, looks the one they
all have to beat, should not be far away, is difficult to
oppose, makes plenty of appeal, will be knocking on the
door, may be the answer, will have many supporters,
should be involved in the finish.*

Going day: 'Torrent is capable of winning this on a
going day but it's guesswork as to what mood he's in.'

The problem is that horses who display *signs of temperament* have more days when they *show little interest*. These horses are said to have **two ways of running**. Hence another very common expression: 'J R Stevenson is very useful *on his day*.'

Going description: The *penetrometer*, compulsory in France, has not really sunk in to many English racecourses, let alone the English consciousness. The official *description* of the going *given* by the clerk of the course is therefore unscientific, and can inspire the wrath of trainers who travel hundreds of miles to find it is inaccurate. 'Good to firm (watering)' is a *description* that handlers of horses with *bad legs* have cause to fear may mean 'hard (as a **road**)'.

Gone: 'He's *gone* on his off-fore.' Jockeys' vernacular when a horse has **broken down**. The participle can also be used more figuratively of horses who are **over the top**, either for their season or their career: 'There are reasons to believe Dancing Lyra can bounce back to form, and punters *putting a line through* his name in the belief that he has "*gone*" should reconsider.' Horses are also said to *go in their coat* in the autumn when they start to grow their winter one: fillies in particular can lose their form when this occurs.

Good effect: Perhaps our imagination, but this phrase seems to be simply a routine way of telling readers who was riding a winner, however good the ride actually was: 'Gino Carenza was *seen to good effect* on the Sue Smith-trained Darab.'

Good speed: Always *shown* early in sprint races. Any prominent horse in a **cavalry charge** is signalled in this way by commentators as they buy time to identify the next runner: 'Also *showing good speed* in the early stages is Selhurstpark Flyer.' The usage is so active that the word *speed* can be dropped entirely: 'Pieter Brueghel is blessed with *good early* and ran a *screamer* on the unfavoured side when second in a big Ripon handicap.'

Go to: 'He had to *go to* 7,500 guineas to keep the horse in the post-race auction'; 'We *went to* €23,000 because we really liked the look of him.' In this simple little verb and preposition hide many complex stories of trainers going way past the maximum they had allowed themselves to secure a horse at auction. A firm of bookmakers is also said to *go* a certain price about a horse, particularly if these odds are out of line with the consensus.

Go to the well: The likely idiom for over-running a horse in the hope of gaining an extra win: 'In retrospect we tried to *go to the well* once too often running him so quickly at Thirsk.' The inverted commas in the next example suggest either that this expression has not been fully absorbed into the lexicon or, more probably in this particular case, that it is almost well known enough to encapsulate meaning by itself: 'I hope we're not "*going to the well*" too often in this one.' Perhaps the metaphor is allied to the proverbial notion that 'you can take a horse to water but you can't make it drink'.

Grand: A *grand* may of course change hands in the betting ring, but the more specific racing usage is when the adjective is applied, almost in homage, to imposing or *scopey* horses: 'His Song and War Of Attrition, both second for Mouse Morris in the Supreme Novices, are *grand* chasing types in appearance.' Irish trainers in particular combine the adjective (see also **super**) with *type* or **sort** to describe a big *old-fashioned* chaser.

Green: A classic racing word, with some classic symptoms to support it: 'He's run very *green* today and stuck his ***head in the air*** when he got in front.' Signs of *greenness* are observed particularly in inexperienced two-year-olds – 'A couple of my youngsters are still very *backward* and *green* but this filly's *battle-hardened* already' – or novice hurdlers: 'He's just a big *green* baby and was *awkward* at his *flights* first time out.'

Green-green screen: Because of the way Betfair recalculates all a trader's positions on a runner in an ante-post market, with winning positions in green and losing positions in red, a *green-green screen* tells the happy tale of a *trader* who has set up his positions in such a way that he will win whatever the outcome. This jingling little rhyme can therefore be used of any set of arbitrage bets where you have contrived such an outcome and can *green up*. Before the *exchanges*, to experience this rewarding, and in the ring pretty unlikely, scenario was to be *on velvet*.

Ground: The *ground* is a daily preoccupation for regular trainers, so that only the state of it needs explaining. However, racing has two usages where the ambit of the word is more circumscribed. In one case the effective meaning is 'a certain measure of *ground*': 'Provided Murphy doesn't *sit* too far *out of his ground* and give the horse *too much to do*, I think he has everything going for him.' In other words, Murphy can *drop* the horse *out*, but must ***keep tabs*** on the other runners by staying within striking distance. In the other case, the original reference would have been to the area of ground before the start: '39 *stood their ground* at yesterday's forfeit stage.' Here the horses referred to did not, as they say, ***defect***.

Guess: 'L'Ami completely *guessed* at that one' – meaning that the horse has not *found a **stride*** before jumping an obstacle. *Guessing* often leads to *pad-dling*. Strangely, jockeys are never accused of *guessing*, although they can be criticised for trying to *make a horse's mind up for him* – see *difference of opinion*.

Gun to the head: Sometimes merely an ornate syn-onym for putting a horse *under* *pressure*, but the phrase may have more specific meanings too, as when a horse is *upped in class*, or *asked* for a *big one*: 'Running Gatwick in a Group 1 is *putting* the *gun to his head*, but he takes his chance'; 'Edredon Bleu always *comes up* for you when you *put* the *gun to his head.*' In questionable taste, as horses are *destroyed* on the racecourse in this way.

H

Hack: 'Sea Bird *hacked up* at Epsom, sweeping into the lead *hard held* inside the final furlong to become one of the easiest Derby winners ever.' This does not mean that Sea Bird expectorated catarrh at Tattenham Corner but that he was absolutely *cruis-ing*, given that a *hack canter* is a very easy one. This is why many stable stars, when they retire, become their trainers' *hacks*. Only very occasionally will you hear racing people use an expression now common in everyday life: 'Rhinestone Cowboy couldn't *hack it* when sent off favourite for the Champion two years ago.'

Hammer: A typical simile, which describes the horses pounding along fast early on in a race: 'He jumps well and stays well, which is important, because they will go like the *hammer.*' Two horses locked in combat can go *at it hammer and tongs*. But it appears some animals have no chance at all against real *tools*: 'Manila and Theatrical couldn't beat Dancing Brave with a *hammer* in Europe.'

Handbrake: 'And Tony Culhane is going to win this one with the *handbrake* firmly *on*.' Not to be tried on the highway but good news on the racetrack, since it means winning with *plenty* in reserve. Less happily, horses can *put on the brakes* when asked to enter the starting stalls or to jump a fence off a long *stride*. Some old *monkeys* will do likewise if they pass the racecourse stables and realise they are being asked to *go out* on another circuit.

Handicapper: An aloof demigod in British racing, the *handicapper* only ever appears in the singular (even though teams of *handicappers* may decide on the weights), which helps to endow this mysterious being with an autocratic aura. Much of the associated vocabulary substantiates this impression. While horses may stay *ahead of the handicapper* or, more brazenly, *defy* him (we assume it is a 'him'), sooner or later they will pay for their Promethean feats by finding themselves 'in the *handicapper's grip*'. But horses can also be *handicappers* – those who tend to run in handicap *grade*. The term tends to be complimentary, indicating experience and guile – 'He jumped like an old *handicapper* today' – although it can be a little ruder if horses are *highly tried*: 'The two making up the field are little more than *handicappers* running round for place money.' And in the United States – in complete contrast to here – it seems everybody is a *handicapper*, because this is their word for any person who takes an interest in the form, be they journalists or punters: 'Plenty of *proficient handicappers* make money relying on the *Daily Racing Form* past performances.'

Handle: A requisite verb when discussing how a
horse might deal with the going or the course: 'How
he *handles* this very soft ground is the only real concern'; 'We just hope he *handles* Chester as he's quite a
big animal.' Of course, there are always some new
trends to have to cope with: 'He should *handle* the
French-style fixed hurdles as we've **schooled** him
extensively.' *Handler* is a less official word for 'trainer',
but *handling* is something a jockey does, and it is usually *strong*.

Hands: 'He came home unopposed *in the hands of*
Martin Dwyer.' In this way you simply avoid having
to say 'ridden by Martin Dwyer' every time. But there
are times when you do want to draw attention to the
soft or *quiet hands* of those sympathetic jockeys who
can **settle** their mounts without having to *fly a kite*.
The quality of the *hands* is of the essence in this next
illustration: 'Francome had *flat-racing hands* and his
ride on Sea Pigeon in the 1981 Champion was the
most breathtaking display of big-race cool since
Lester's Derby on Sir Ivor in 1968.' A horse is measured at the shoulder in *hands* (units of four inches),
although references to these measurements in general
racing journalism are rare unless the horse is a very
grand *sort* indeed, like *eighteen-hands* Party Politics.

Hands and heels: *Assistance* given by a jockey
without his *resorting* to the whip. So if a horse has
only had to be *ridden out hands and heels* to win, he
has done so relatively easily. There are now special
hands-and-heels races for apprentices, to help them
learn to **punch** *out* a horse in this way – often benefi-
cial because over-reliance on the whip can *unbalance*
a horse during a finish and *sour* him for future
engagements. Mind you, in the heat of battle some of
the **boys** forget they are not allowed to resort to the
beater.

Handy: In racing tends not to mean 'useful' but *up with the pace*: 'Kristensen was always *lying* up *handy*'; 'Geraghty had always *kept* Essex *handy* and ***produced*** him in the straight.' Though some stable lads, especially those who box or attend the ***Lesters***, are known to be a bit *handy* for their size.

Hang: Although there are several other ways of noting the fact that a horse has not kept to a straight line, especially in a finish, *hanging* is the canonical term, seen regularly in race-reading: '*hung* left run-in, *all out*'; '*hung* badly right under pressure'. Beyond Britain and Ireland, a horse who *hangs* can be said by English-speakers to *bear in* or *out*, although Australians may prefer to perk up the standard terminology: 'On the turn she was *hanging out* like grandma's teeth.'

Hanging about: One of those phrases which, in the logic of the sport, only appears in the negative: 'There was *no hanging about* in this Grade 2 contest, with Cloudy Bays and Take The Stand taking the field along at a *cracking **clip*** from the outset.' When a jockey riding a horse who needs an ***end-to-end*** gallop has to *cut out* his own running, you may hear the commentator say: 'Mick Fitzgerald on Etendard Indien is rightly *ensuring* there'll be *no hanging about*.' When they do actually *hang about*, reach for other terms like ***tactical*** and ***muddling***.

Happening too quickly: This phrase allows a more angular view of a horse struggling to *go the pace*: 'Mandarin Spirit, who found things *happening* a bit *too quickly* for him over 6 furlongs last time, could be ***called*** the winner a long way out over this ***trip***.' Naturally, if it is a jockey reporting back, *quickly* can be shortened to *quick*. See also ***taken off his feet***.

Hard-luck story: When looking back on a race, particularly a big handicap on the flat, reporters always seem keen to give a consolation award for this: 'Perhaps the *hard-luck story* of the contest involved Hadeer, who was *squeezed for room* two out and could not find a *clear **passage*** after.'

Hard on the steel: This most emphatically does not mean 'pedal to the metal' but the opposite: 'In a sensational King George, Mick Kinane won *hard on the steel.*' In other words, *on the bridle*, without the horse ever letting go of the bit.

Hats: These come *off* during or after a famous victory, as in Peter O'Sullevan's by now celebrated commentary on Red Rum's historic third National triumph: 'It's *hats off* and a tremendous reception – you've never heard one like it at Liverpool.' Racing people still actually wear *hats*, when they are not throwing them as far as they can – Dawn Run's reception after her Gold Cup providing another example.

Headgear: The aid will be noted in running commentary more for identification purposes – 'Arctic Call's on the right *in the headgear*' – than to comment on whether the blinkers, hood, visor, eyeshield or cheekpieces are actually working.

Head in the air: If a horse puts his *head in the air* in a finish, this can just be a sign of *greenness*, but it tends to suggest that he is ***irresolute*** and not one to be trusted ***implicitly***. A distinctly *ungenuine sort* will invite something more imaginative: 'Even if Point Of Dispute does respond to the *feminine touch*, expect to see his *Exocet-style head-spinning* once **asked** for an *effort.*' If horses have their *head in the air* early in a race, it may be a sign they are **pulling** too hard (see ***fly a kite***) and commentators sometimes note this:

'Hopefully Leo's Lucky Star will *drop his head.*'
Jockeys, on the other hand, can be said to get their
heads down in a finish, which can be awkward if
the last fence is ***dolled off***: 'In a *heads-down finish*
Johnson was forced to manoeuvre his mount swiftly
left around the markers.'

Head in chest: One of the classic clichés, like ***steering job***, for a win achieved with the minimum of
fuss. Conveys the idea that the horse is full of running at the finish and is winning *under restraint*.

Head in front: 'After six frustrating seconds on the
flat, Softway finally got her *head in front* over hurdles
at Enghien.' Used in describing a close finish, it is
more pertinently applied whenever a horse ends a
long losing sequence or, as in the above example, a
bout of ***seconditis***.

Head waiter: Some jockeys become particularly
famous for riding a *waiting race* and the most nerveless rider of each generation may become known as
the *head waiter*. Harry Wragg's arrival on the ***scene***
on Felstead in the 1928 Derby first gave rise to the
wordplay, although *swooping* as ***fast and late*** as he
did that day is probably not advisable for silver service staff when dishing out the sprouts.

Heap: Horses can *land in a heap* if they overjump and
lose momentum after a fence, but the more common
usage is to describe a field *finishing in a heap*. Such
blanket finishes invariably cast a doubt on the value
of the form: 'They came home *in a heap* and there
must be question marks about how the form will *work
out.*'

Here comes: In live commentary, if there is a short-
priced ***hold-up horse*** in the field that many punters

will have backed, this is almost automatically the way of announcing the first sign of a serious forward move: '*Here comes* Cape Royal down the wide outside.' Sadly for punters, this is not a guarantee that the *hotpot* will keep on coming.

Himself: Only one horse can be referred to as *Himself*: Arkle. But the word is employed all the time when trainers are talking about a horse's well-being: 'He's very well *in himself*'; 'He's on *good terms with himself*'; 'He pulled up a little bit stiff *in himself*.' The first usage, in particular, may seem tautologous, but handlers of racehorses do seem to think in terms of their charges not being themselves: 'Rimell feels Oneway has only just *come to himself*'; 'If they're not right when they come over from France, you have to let them *come to themselves*.' So prevalent is the idea in racing that it can be applied to trainers rather than their **inmates**, as in this example seen in the *Racing Post*: 'Martin Pipe has *looked* particularly *well* and on *good terms with himself* recently.'

His: If a horse duly wins a certain category of race for which he or she is then no longer qualified (or, at least, not on such good **terms**), the possessive comes into its own: 'He won *his* maiden quite nicely'; 'She won *her* **bumper** in good style.' Conspicuous also when it's a matter of shaking your head about a bad run: 'Exit Smiling just didn't run *his* race'; 'Lyca Ballerina didn't show *her* running today.'

Hit the crossbar: Imported from football to describe a horse who has *done everything but win*: 'Perouse *hit the crossbar* a few times last term but looks a **different horse** now.' Other parts of the woodwork are as likely to be struck if you are a close second: 'Be Upstanding *hit the post* for the third race in succession.' Another football formula is *penalty kick*, to describe a very good opportunity for a horse given the conditions of the race.

Hobdaying: A process for curing *wind* defects, named after Sir Frederick Hobday, who pioneered the technique for removing the vocal chords. First time listeners to John Hamner's commentary might be forgiven for assuming that the procedure is readily available on the National Health Service. We also had to do a double take when we saw the headline: 'Rigmarole has had a *second wind* operation' – before deciding it must have been what we first thought.

Hock deep: Nothing to do with grape-harvesting along the Rhine, but still very soft going (even if not quite *bottomless*).

Hold-up horse: Not the same thing as a *bridle horse*, as he is actually expected to *find* something off the bit. Backing an animal with this style of running, which the Americans call *closing*, means that your heart will be in your mouth if the *traffic* is busy.

Home: In racing, as once upon a time in elementary board games, *home* means 'the finish'. But *home* is also where so many racing stories start, in the form of the *reports* that emanate from the stables and the *gallops*. *For home* is the presiding term for use at the race-course, where the runners *turn for home*, *go for home*, *kick for home*, *strike for home* and generally do any-thing within the Rules of Racing to *get home*. *At home* is the phrase that sits easy in the training context: 'We have done as much as we can with My Paris *at home* and he's been *working* well'; 'She never *shows* us too much *at home*.' For the rest, we may want to concern ourselves about the *good home* racehorses will need to find when they have finished racing, or racing has finished with them. Which reminds us that *home and* *hosed* has done such long service in racing that it has begun to look for a *home* in other sports.

Hoodoo: 'Wayward Lad! Can he bury his Cheltenham *hoodoo*?' Some jockeys and horses seem to become *course specialists* on the score of poor performance: 'Russ Garritty, who hadn't ridden a winner at Musselburgh for nearly seven years, broke his *hoodoo* by *landing a double*'; 'Kemp has named Newcastle *invader* Impaler as the main threat but is hoping the Toowoomba track *hoodoo* will work against the four-year-old.' For all the attempts to account for form by reference to long-term trends, recourse to *systems* and study of all conceivable criteria, racing still has a place for the superstitious explanation.

Horlicks: In a sport where even some of the animals can be partial to a **Mackeson** or two, allusions to the bedtime drink are perhaps inevitably contemptuous. References to *Horlicks* hardly advertise the product, since they most often portray a jumping mistake – 'He made a right *horlicks* of the second last' – or situations where the race becomes very **tactical**: 'In retrospect, the three-runner race with no *pace on* was always going to be a *horlicks* of a contest.'

Horseman: This is a unisex term for a jockey who **gets on well** with his or her mount and has all-round riding skills. Special admiration is reserved for great *pieces* of *horsemanship*, such as a miraculous recovery at a fence or a successful effort to **settle** a headstrong individual. Note that, in America, if someone is described as a *horseman*, they could be any of the connections, not just the jockey.

Hot: This adjective can describe a competitive race but also a *fizzy* horse: 'Centaurus is a little bit *hot* and can get a bit too **keen** so we are just going to feel our way with him.' But its more systematic usage is to mean 'fashionable' when referring to a sire: 'The colt, now a most valuable son of *hot* sire Redoute's Choice, has been conservatively valued in the millions.' *Bloodstock agents* can sometimes pick up bargains when the heat is off: 'We got him for a nice price because Lyphard had just gone a bit *cold* at the time.'

HQ: In Britain, this invariably means Newmarket for the summer *game* and Cheltenham for the winter one. This pairing may be slightly inconsistent in that Newmarket is the country's leading training centre, Lambourn its equivalent for jumps, and Cheltenham is where *all roads lead* for the Festival whereas, although Newmarket stages two classics, Ascot (or, to make it temporarily more confusing at the time of writing, York) is the home of British flat racing's most significant single meeting. What is certain is that it's a degree smarter to say *HQ* than 'Headquarters'.

Hunt: Although the *Royal Hunt Cup* is a famous race over a straight mile, a *hunter* tends to mean something slow (especially if he is the *whipper-in*), and a rider will *hunt round* when he is trying to *drop* a horse *out* before the race *gets **serious***. The advice of Dan Moore for the National is typical in this respect: 'At Liverpool you want to *hunt* and *hunt* and *hunt* until you come onto the racecourse and then you can start thinking about being a jockey.'

I

Ideas: Perhaps strangely, the only parties who are acknowledged to have *ideas* in racing are not innovative trainers, enterprising jockeys or forward-thinking industry officials but *squiggle horses*: 'Upgrade has less on his plate than in recent starts but has *his own ideas* about the *game* and may also dislike the ground.'

Idling: 'Despite *idling* on the run-in at Navan last time, Cane Brake stuck to his task when it really mattered in the closing stages.' This is a good example of the way *idling* does not necessarily indicate that a horse is lazy, but that he thinks he has *done enough* once he *hits the front*. Indeed, it is extremely unusual for any horse except the leader to be described as *idling*.

Ill-fated: The invariable adjective for a racehorse *killed in action* and momentarily resurrected in discussion: 'Even the *ill-fated* Gloria Victis would not have won the Gold Cup, although he was running much better than most novices in the race.'

Implicitly: 'Admiral Peary is not one to *rely* on *implicitly*.' An adverb beloved of Timeform which in fact serves as an explicit warning to punters that a particular horse may have *more temperament than ability*, and will almost certainly not give his *true running*.

Imposing: An adjective reserved either for strapping chasers, or for the fences they are asked to jump. A fence can be at the same time *imposing* and *inviting*, if it is big but *well presented*. Aintree, Haydock Park and Cheltenham always seem to earn the unofficial awards for fence-building.

In: 'He finished a disappointing third *in* Thurles last time'; 'After his win *in* Galway, he is looking to follow up here today.' For Irish people this is a perfectly natural prepositional choice which can evoke in British

minds images of the horse running round the streets
of the town in question. This side of the Irish Sea, connections prefer to speak of a horse that has won *at*
Chepstow, but you will also hear that an animal per-
forms *around* Uttoxeter (as though he always does well
in Staffordshire). This usage is no doubt encouraged by
the longer *circuits* of a National Hunt course. See also
round here.

In and out: Not a reference to *weaving* (see **vices**),
but to inconsistent form: 'Barrow Drive has been
very *in and out* this season'; 'He was very *in and out*
last term but he's matured physically and I expect
him to do well this time.'

Informative: Races are particularly *informative*
when they are official or unofficial **trials** for bigger
races later. The implication sometimes is that *informative* races of this kind might not be the best betting
mediums.

Inmate: Racehorses lead regimented lives, a fact to
which the common metaphor of stable-as-prison pays
tribute: 'By using the pool and the automatic exerci-
sers, we manage to get most *inmates* out of their stables
twice a day, breaking up their *confinement* as much as
possible.' But the noun can also be used very routinely
and without trace of irony: 'Our Vic, Control Man and
Bannow Strand are all exciting Pond House *inmates*.'
The French equivalent, *pensionnaire*, translates as
'boarder' or 'resident' (what *inmate* used to mean in
English), and may be more suitable given the *five-star
treatment* that racehorses are alleged to receive
compared to many other breeds.

In season: Racing's way of saying 'having her time of
the month'. If you hear that a mare is *on*, this is likely
to mean *on the bridle* rather than 'on heat'.

Instructions: While some trainers consider briefing the jockey on tactics to be unnecessary – 'The good ones don't take any notice anyway' – such *instructions* become particularly important when connections have been summoned before the stewards to defend themselves from the charge of **schooling** *in public*: 'The jockey reported that his *instructions* were to "**settle** the gelding, give him **plenty** of **daylight**, to get him *travelling* and to make late progress *if possible*". Which can be interpreted as: 'The trainer told me the horse was **not off** today, that I should get him completely *detached* and that I should only start **scrubbing along** near the stands to make it look less obvious.'

In the know: 'Over £400 was matched at around 190-210 on Betfair, suggesting somebody was *in the know*.' *Savants* in racing (see **face**) can be *well informed* or *well connected*, but more commonly they will be *in the know*. Means 'in on the secret' more than 'knowledgeable' and was a phrase much used by the late Graham Rock in his reports from the ring.

Interference: The technical term for any incident where one horse impedes another. Whether such *interference* is *accidental* will be material to the jockey, because he will be suspended if it is deemed to be his fault: 'Bog Trotter was very badly *interfered with* at the **distance**, but the stewards decided not to reverse the placings.'

Into: The required preposition in some common racing phrases. When a trainer is trying to get a horse **cherry-ripe** for a future target he will often confess the following: 'We really need to *get a run into* him if we're going to get him to Cheltenham.' During a race, jockeys will try to get a *breather* or a *blow into* their mounts. They can also get *into* the **roots** over jumps, and *into* **traffic** *trouble* on the level.

Irons: What stirrups always become when they have been *lost*.

Irresolute: A word which, though dropping out of use, is conserved in the terse and unforgiving prose of Timeform: 'MIDNIGHT CREEK: . . . *tried* in cheekpieces/visor, tongue tied last time; *irresolute*.'

It: The pronoun *it* is not permissible in racing commentary when describing a horse which (or perhaps *who*) may have qualities and flaws attributable to gender. Furthermore, even unsentimental professionals (and lexicographers) tend to think of racehorses as if they were people rather than things. When, however, exasperation has got the better of a punter, the personal pronoun can give way to a cruel, inanimate one: '*It* just won't leave the stalls. What a *mule*.'

J

Jar: Firm going can *jar up* horses, which may just mean that they are left a little *sore*; but the term can also be used more euphemistically of an animal that has all but **broken down**. You will therefore hear trainers say: 'I'll walk the course first thing and if there's any *jar* in the ground I'll pull him out.'

Jig-jog: An extreme form of a horse being *on his **toes***, when he gets so excited he breaks into a little trot on the spot. *Jig-jogging* in the paddock can be a sign of his becoming *buzzed up* by the occasion, although for some horses it is, or was, part of their nature: 'When he was young, Forest Gunner was very *headstrong*, a bit of a *nutter* who *jig-jogged* everywhere, was *fractious* all the time and had to be at the front of the *string*.'

Jock off: To remove a rider from a previously *retained* ride. So bitter an experience for the rider replaced that it is no surprise it sounds like an expletive.

John Wayne: Representative of a riding style slightly less *short* than the current fashion: 'Watching a bunch of amateurs riding *longer than John Wayne* on some right slow old *boats* in the Foxhunters is not everybody's cup of tea.' There are other pejorative terms available: 'In this high-speed hurdle race company, Pat Taafe's upright *Master of Foxhounds* style of riding was shown up.' However, jockeys who ride *straightback* can sometimes have the last laugh when *horsemanship* is at a premium.

Jolly: Vernacular for favourite, seemingly designed to reflect the good mood of *favourite backers* when it comes in, but anything can happen: 'There was a discernible cheer from the layers when the *jolly unseated* at the last.' The derivation is unknown but it is interesting that the *OED* cites an example from 1869 where to *jolly* means 'to make a sham bid at a horse auction'. At least this practice, if not the expression, is alive and well.

Judge: The official responsible for determining the placings of a race and the *official distances* between the placed horses. Therefore, in a very tight finish, the commentator's alternative to '*Photo!*' is to say, 'That's one for the *judge*.' If even the print of the finish leaves no room for doubt, everyone at the course will be *waiting on* the *judge* until the result is announced. And if there are several photo-finishes at one meeting, the *judge* is invariably said to have had a *busy day*. Perhaps, by the standards of a stipendiary steward, he has. Because that is where he sits (at most courses anyway), the *judge* helps, this time in an unpaid capacity, to identify the point of the course which will be the winning line *next time round* (or possibly five times round at Fakenham): 'As they pass the *judge* with a circuit to run . . .' And, in a common expression, his being put out is an indication that a horse has put his **head in front**: 'Little strength in depth here, and only Plummet had *troubled the judge* recently.'

Juice: The opposite of *jar*: 'There's a bit more *juice* in the going today, which is my one concern, as he likes to hear his hooves *rattle*.' *Ease* and *give* are alternatives when trainers are reporting softer conditions underfoot: 'With the overnight rain there'll be some *give* in the ground, which will suit my fellow.' *Juice* can also mean petrol, especially when you notice that the **tank** is close to **empty**.

Jump off: Flat racers also *jump*, in the sense that they *jump off* from the stalls: 'Council Member *jumped off* into his customary lead'; 'Neil Callan *jumped* Amber Glory *off* smartly.' The *off* is distinctive unless the context is clarified further, as in: 'The horse *jumped well* from stall 7.' More contentious is any allegation that a jockey *jumped off* a horse deliberately, motivated by fear or greed: 'Anybody who knows me will agree I would never *jump off* a horse.'

K

Keen: 'He's a *bit keen*': from time immemorial trainers have been saying this to jockeys, before they give them the **leg-up**, with varying degrees of understatement. Unless they have evidence to the contrary, the rider will tend to translate as follows: 'He's a raving lunatic who nobody can *sit on* at home and he'll no doubt *run away* with me down to the start and *pull my arms out* from the *off*, then I'll get *bollocked* for not settling him when he *stops as if he's been shot.*' *Keenness* is therefore not a good thing in a racehorse, as he will be too *keen* for *his own good.* And yet racing people can quickly criticise animals for not being *keen* enough: 'Cabin Fever looked *none too keen* when third at Kempton.' This is a very common and understated way of saying that a horse is not *enjoying himself.* But never say a horse is *really hating it* unless there are excuses like *bottomless* ground.

Keep something for himself: An endearingly euphemistic phrase for a horse who is experienced enough not to *go through with his effort*: 'He's becoming a bit of a *character* and tends to *keep something for himself* at the end of his races nowadays.' Note that the horse in question never *keeps* or *saves* 'a lot' or 'everything' for himself, and therefore the jockey has licence to give him the full *treatment*.

Keep tabs: A well-worn expression in many walks of life; in racing, it registers the fact that a horse has kept close enough to the *principals* to remain *in contention*. How worthwhile the surveillance will be usually depends on how much horse you have *under* you: 'Look at Willie Carson *keeping tabs* on Pat Eddery and ready to *pounce*'; 'Although he *kept tabs* on the first two until the straight the horse was very tired when he fell at the last.'

Keep up: Perhaps strangely, it is rare for a commentator to remark that a horse cannot 'keep up' with other runners; instead he will be unable to *go the gallop* or *live* with the pace. The verbal phrase is instead used for the way jockeys *keep* their mounts *up* to their work. Though some exceptional horses probably find the *assistance* of their jockeys unhelpful as they sustain the pace: 'Monksfield could be guaranteed to *keep it up* in the face of *whip frenzies* from his riders.' More ***moderate*** *plodders* are said to *keep on* (going) once they come under pressure.

Kickback: 'She *resented* the *kickback* last time and we'll try to ride her more forcefully today.' An expression which is likely to fall out of use as quickly as it came in, given that Polytrack is replacing other *all-weather* surfaces, and much less *dirt* is kicked up into the faces of ***hold-up horses***. If you are politically incorrect you can describe a jockey who has been *in rear* throughout a race and is therefore covered in *kickback* as looking like *something* out of the *Black and White Minstrel Show* (the same phrase used to be applied to jump jockeys removing their goggles after a *slog* in the ***mud***).

Kill himself: 'I don't think he *killed himself* at Leopardstown and I would be tempted to put blinkers on him next time.' In view of the risks involved in either code of racing, perhaps not the most enlightened way of saying a horse has not been *putting it all in*.

Kinks: Used of horses to describe behavioural rather than physical defects: 'The winning trainer noted that the colt has his *kinks*, and is not one to trust ***implicitly***.' There is nothing untoward about the adjective, which is understood as a technical term in racing: 'She's very *kinky* but she's got lots of form in this ***company***.'

Knackered: Despite (perhaps because of) connotations of the *knacker's yard* or *van*, frequently used in racing, and conceivably with some degree of subtlety in the actual phrasing: 'Nottage has *knackered himself up* on this firm ground'; 'Steve Smith Eccles looks *absolutely knackered*.'

Knocking: In Ireland this word sometimes appears to be a variant of *effing* – 'Emotional Moment is *knocking* each-way *value* at 12/1' – but we believe Dermot Weld is referring to his charge's *action* in this interview: 'Elusive Double is a nice *hard-knocking* colt who is working well.'

Knock on the door: Not the bailiffs calling again, but a horse on the verge of breaking through to success. Applicable also to an emerging trainer, or one trying to end a barren spell, as in the following variation: 'Matt Gingell was so close to *opening the door* after 107 days in the *cold* when New Perk and Alfhalo both finished second.'

Know: 'The fact that Harchibald got close before putting his *head in the air* simply underlined the excellent ride Carberry gave him – namely he didn't *know* he was *in a race* until the *shadow* of the post.' Just as a *thinker* is to be distrusted, so horses need to be shielded from knowledge, otherwise they may well *keep something for themselves*. Not that knowledge seems to help connections or punters very much.

Know the time of day: 'Willie Mullins's record in the *Festival bumper* is second to none and the owners *know the time of day* as well, having saddled Florida Pearl to win twice at the Festival.' A cliché for professionalism and experience, sometimes applied in contexts that are not immediately obvious: 'And completing tonight's preview panel are two Irish jockeys who certainly *know what time of day* it is.'

Knuckle: What horses do *on landing* when they cannot get their *undercarriage* out in time. Seemingly, it is possible to make a *miraculous recovery* from *knuckling*, whereas *crumpling* definitely entails a fall or *unseated*: 'Many horses have *knuckled on landing* at

Becher's – Rhyme 'N' Reason and Miinnehoma among them – and gone on to win the National.'

L

Ladies: *Ladies' Day* at Royal Ascot is copied by racecourses elsewhere when they have run out of other public relations ideas (see *facilities*). The helpful cashiers for the *Nanny* used to be compared to *Butlin's Redcoats* but, post Chris de Burgh, are sometimes marketed as *Ladies in red*. Punters *looking for a little romance* are, however, likely to be disappointed.

Land the odds: While the phrase can convey the fact that connections have successfully *had a touch*, it also finds expression in a neutral narrative idiom to indicate that a horse won as favourite: 'Forty Licks *landed the odds* at Clonmel by ten lengths from Insan Express, then followed up *in style* by the same margin at Leopardstown.'

Languish: As in other sports, trainers or jockeys will tend to *languish* in the lower reaches of their respective tables, but the verb has been customised in racing for horses *out* of the handicap: 'Non So is *languishing* on 9st 2lb and the minimum weight is 10st 4lb.'

Lay out: 'I *laid him out* for a race at Towcester at the start of the season and thought he was a certainty, but he was beaten half a length.' This does not mean that the trainer planted a right cross on his horse, or injected him with tranquillisers, to keep him restrained before the race he wanted to win, but that he has specifically *prepared* his charge for one race, usually a handicap, ignoring other opportunities.

Horses can also be *laid out off* the pace (or *up* with it) in the race itself, while bookmakers by profession *lay* bets, and by necessity *lay* them *off* along the **rails** if their potential liabilities are dangerously high.

Lead: Horses are *led up* by their lads before a race and *led in*, often by their connections, if they win it. When we come to the noun, *getting a lead* does not mean 'taking the lead', as the following example will show: 'I *got* a great *lead off* Gary Carter on Prince Aaron and I always thought my filly would **get up.**' Horses are **blissfully unaware** of all these prepositions. But see also **off**.

Left: In race-reading, horses are *left* in two contexts: at the start if they get off to a *bad one* and towards the finish if the fall of another horse promotes them to a better position: 'Held up, progress 13th, soon beaten, *left* poor third last.'

Leg: 'He's developed a *touch of a leg* and I'm not going to risk him just yet.' These casual-sounding statements manage to avoid the word 'bad', which would be enough to confirm that the one bad leg was rendering the horse seriously lame. On the other hand, if a horse has *bad legs*, usually *bad front legs*, this is an indication of historical **problems** that require careful handling, but that do not preclude the horse winning again, even if the said legs won't *stand* much racing. During a race, *legs* means 'more pace': 'I thought they might *have the legs* of him bringing him back to two miles on a **sharp** track.' *Legless*, as in other sports, is a synonym for 'very tired', though clever jumpers can sometimes *find a leg* even in these circumstances to prevent themselves falling.

Legendary: Customarily appended to the name of J. P. McManus (though Sir Alex Ferguson may have a few other words in mind). Gamblers seem, perhaps unfairly, more likely to attract the epithet than jockeys or trainers, maybe because their achievements are not as verifiable. Only horses, though, can be truly *legendary*.

Leg-up: Trainers really do *give* their jockeys a *leg-up* into the saddle and, as night follows day, jockeys *take* a *leg-up*. The idiom arises, though, when *leg-up* is used as synonymous with 'ride'. For example: 'Richard Ford *gave* Buchanan the *leg-up* on Forest Gunner in the Grand Sefton.' Jockeys may indeed express gratitude to trainers for *putting them up* or, in some cases, simply putting up with them.

Lengthen: Can be used of odds, reins or strides. Most idiomatic, though, when the last of these nouns disappears from the phrase: 'Shape Up *lengthened readily* to win by two lengths.'

Lesters: The *Racing Post* has pronounced, with almost divine authority, that the jockeys' annual awards ceremony that goes under this name 'was, is and always will be about boogieing, booze and black eyes'. We have commented in the Preface on the importance of the three Rs for an appreciation of racing.

Let: At the climax of a race, jockeys are said to *let* their horses *down*, which does not mean they are **disappointing** them, but that they are asking them to *stride out*: '"Come on, Norman," I'm muttering under my breath. "*Let him down*. **Press the button**. Let him go"'. Sometimes in these circumstances a horse will refuse to *stretch out*: 'Fergal Lynch reported that Sovereign State had *run flat* and would not *let himself down.*' Confusingly, *let down* is also a synonym for **rough off**: 'We've *let* him *down* for the season as he probably won't *get his ground* again.' We hope the horse wasn't too deflated by this last experience.

Lick: Used narratively for the speed of the gallop (usually a *strong* one): 'Certainly a *good lick* on here with New Halen to the fore.' For extra emphasis, there is an onomatopoeic version: 'They were going absolutely *lickety-split* from flagfall.'

Lift over the line: 'Champion jockey McCoy *lifted* Mini Sensation *over the line.*' Implausible in view of their respective weights (however mini Mini Sensation might be), but the verb lends itself figuratively to praise a Herculean effort by the jockey. If you want to emphasise a horse's superiority you can conjure up a similar image: 'Arkle was passed on the run-in by Dormant, a horse whom in the normal course of events he could have *picked up and carried.*'

Limpet: The preferred crustacean when you're reaching for a simile to testify to the *adhesive powers* of a jump jockey: 'Russ Garritty stuck like a *limpet* to spare ride Lord Of The River when he **blundered** badly two out.'

Little: Tends to be a measure in racing parlance of quality rather than of size, for which there are several other expressions (see **pony**). Helpful when describing races **moderate** horses might tackle in the future, with the implication that these races will be of very low class at one of the **gaffs**, and will be so undemanding as to be within the horse's compass: 'She's *shown me enough* today to suggest she can win a *little race* somewhere.' When overheard in the atmospheric *owners' and trainers' bar* at Fakenham, it is difficult to surmise exactly where this *somewhere* might be.

London to a brick on: A way of saying 'very long odds-on' which was a signature phrase of the much-missed Australian race-caller Ken Howard. This probably constitutes even less generous odds than the *magic figure* of 1.01 on Betfair, the shortest possible price a horse can trade on the *exchanges*. When a horse *dominates* the betting in this way, at least there are other ways of trying to stimulate interest in some cities: 'Perth's star three-year-old Plastered has *stifled* betting on Saturday's WATC Derby at Belmont Park to such an extent that he can be backed in doubles with local AFL teams West Coast Eagles and Fremantle Dockers.'

Lonely: Unless their charge is a particularly nervous *sort* who is comforted by having a sheep for company in the horsebox, trainers only worry about horses being *lonely* when their *splendid isolation* in a race causes them to stop *concentrating* in front: 'River Phantom was just getting a bit *lonely* in front on the run-in.' Though certain **confirmed** *trailblazers* will *sulk* if they are not *left alone* in the *van*.

Look: One of the signs that a horse in either code may be a **thinker** is a tendency to *look about* or *around* (although on the flat this may simply be a sign of *greenness* in a two-year-old). Such a horse can benefit from the *application* of *blinkers*. Perhaps curiously, it is also not advisable for a horse to *look* too hard at his obstacles: 'Epitre seemed the winner going to the last but *took* a *good look* at the hurdle and *fluffed* it, which lost him vital momentum.' This set phrase always indicates hesitation, even near refusal.

Look after: Could well appear in an explanation to the stewards for a **tender** ride, as follows: 'My **instructions** today were to *hold him* together and *look after* him on the ground.' But more common as a reflexive verb used of a horse who **keeps something for himself**: 'He tends to *look after* himself in his races these days.'

Loose: Characterises soft going at the other end of the scale to *gluey*. Although the turf can be so *loose* as to be dangerous, usually such conditions are preferable because horses can more easily *go through* ground where they are *kicking up* a proper *sod*: 'The ground was very *holding* when Queens Square ran third last time: Julian *got off* and told us that he would prefer it *looser.*'

Lord of all he surveyed: Grandiose, if not pompous, expression to describe a jockey employing *hold-up* tactics who has *enough* horse **under** him to **cover** every move easily: 'Carberry got him into a proper *working rhythm* and *sat* at the back of the field, *lord of all he surveyed.*' Carberry may even have had time in these circumstances to read the poem by William Cowper from which the phrase seems originally to have emerged.

Lose caste: *Caste* is not something you are allowed to talk about much these days, but it is perfectly acceptable in racing when describing a brave performance by a placed horse: 'Goodtime George *lost no caste* in defeat and was simply beaten by a better horse on the day.' In these circumstances you can also say that the horse was *far from disgraced* or *lost nothing* in defeat. Here is another alternative provided by Rodney Masters: 'Neither Azertiyoup or Well Chief *shed any kudos* in defeat.' The phrase *lose caste* seems to have first appeared in Regency England to indicate a person's descent down the social scale; it is therefore appropriate in the context of thoroughbreds who race in particular grades related to how much *class* they have shown in the past.

Lose his way: A horse can *lose his way*, which does not mean that his box arrives in Bangor-on-Sea rather than Bangor-on-Dee (though that will not help) nor that his jockey takes the wrong course. The usage is designed for animals who posted good early form only to prove **disappointing**: 'After showing early promise, Rocket Force seems to have completely *lost his way*: he has talent but hasn't **sparkled** at all.' Conversely, *progressive* animals are often said to be *going the right way*.

Lot: 'Hills picked up the injury *first lot* when a horse reared up on him'; 'On Wednesdays I *ride work* for Mr Walwyn, usually *second and third lots*.' Most large training establishments send their horses out for home work in batches which are always called *lots* (definite article not required).

Lower the colours: Idiomatic for 'to defeat', as in 'Only Oneway has managed to *lower the colours* of Colonel Frank this season.' Possibly prompted by the military suggestion in the defeated horse's name on this occasion, though reporters seem to be trained to ignore this kind of stimulus. When a favourite is *turned over*, Australian journalists are regularly attracted to a different metaphor: 'Top weight Messiaen *lowered the boom* on Power Hunt ($1.85 fav), holding on to a long head.' The word *boom* can therefore stand on its own to denote what the British would probably call a *good thing*: 'Some big two-year-old *booms* went bust.'

Lucky last: A nice little alliterative title bestowed by punters (and consequently by journalists) on the last race of the day, which, for the majority of us, is a chance to *get out of jail*. Therefore also known as the *get-out* or *getting-out stakes*, even if the race is an *impossible* handicap. Usually won by an *unthought of* 33/1 shot whom nobody in your party has backed.

Lump: Betting vernacular for putting the *money down*, with a choice of prepositions: 'It seemed everybody was *lumping in* as the 10/1 available in the morning soon disappeared'; 'Powerscourt has *bags of talent* but isn't **straightforward** and is not one to *lump on*.' As for the noun, horses high in the handicap are said to give *lumps* of weight away.

Luxury: An apparently archaic expression to describe a good **racing weight** that is less than a horse is used to carrying: 'If Arkle does contest the Grand Steeplechase de Paris, he will carry the *luxury weight* of 10st 1lb.'

M

Machine: 'Ruby got off Kauto Star and said he was a *machine*. End of story.' Indeed, this kind of description tends to brook no argument – it is conferred on horses who seem to gallop remorselessly with no **quirks** or **kinks**. Sometimes the *maintenance work* is important: 'Obviously we missed a little time with the weather, so the *screws* are not totally tight – the Derby is still a ways away.' We should remember, though, that one of the most regular excuses for a **disappointing** run is that 'horses are not *machines*'.

Mackeson: Certain sponsored handicaps are so lodged in the racegoing public's psyche that even when the product advertised is out of fashion and the race has long since assumed another official title, the old name survives, unrenewed, at every **renewal**. Thus the *Mackeson Gold Cup*, the first big handicap of the jumps season, despite enduring successive reincarnations as the 'Murphys', the 'Thomas Pink', and now the 'Paddy Power', remains *the Mackeson* for many people. The same is true of the last big handicap, which lives on as *the Whitbread* even if the race has been rebranded as the 'Betfred Gold Cup'. If the longest-running sponsorship we can think of ever came to an end, the big staying chase run at Newbury each November would still be referred to as *the Hennessy*, in the same way that the 'Tote Gold Trophy', held on the same course in February, is called *the Schweppes* by anybody old enough to remember the previous embodiment. What does it say about punters that in all these cases it is a drink that provides the hangover of the previous name?

Made him look good: 'He even *carried* the Princess Royal once, in a handicap at Newmarket – I expect he *made her look good* too.' A phrase where the social tensions between connections do work their way through. It tends to be used by a *blunt* handler after an amateur riders' race, with the subtext that he probably shouldn't be wasting such *good rides* on such poor riders.

Main track: In North America, this is not some way of distinguishing between glamour tracks and *leaky-roof* venues, but instead tells you the races will be run on dirt not grass: 'Cape Hope has established herself as one of the best 3-year-old turf fillies in the country. Friday, she could make a case for being one of the best, period, when she returns to the *main track* at Oaklawn Park.' On standard *ovals* the grass course (if there is one) is always the *inner track*, so that if a specialist on that surface tries the other she looks to *carry over* on the dirt. The only exception to the rule in North America is at Woodbine, in Toronto, where our Canadian cousins maintain the best traditions of the *turf*.

Make all: 'It was a brave attempt to *make all* but she just couldn't hold on.' The *running* is so readily understood that phrases like *made all* or *made most* are staples of potted race-reading.

Make up: 'Len Lungo is convinced Wild Cane Ridge will *make up into* a decent *staying chaser*'; 'Formerly trained by David Elsworth, Cape Of Good Hope is *making up into* a smart performer in Hong Kong.' The *up* seems to be characteristic of and obligatory in racing parlance, perhaps because an element of growing up is fundamental to these projections of career development, perhaps because *make up* has a specific sense, first recorded by the *OED* in 1794, of 'getting a horse in good condition for sale'. See also **train on**. Racing saddles are *made up* when they have girths, stirrup leathers and *irons* attached.

Make use of: 'He's very **keen** and I had to *make* so much *use of* him as he's basically a three-miler'; 'Admittedly he weakened last time in handicap *company*, but *a lot of use* was *made* of him that day.' Note how jockeys never merely 'use' what is **under** them but *make use* of it. They will earn praise or criticism depending on whether the forcing *tactics* work or not.

Man: Trainers are very keen to see their charges mature as quickly as possible and so often hope a particular experience will help *make a man* of their horse. An observation like '*gelding him* has really helped to *make* him a *man*' would be bizarre, but not unfeasible. If you believe a horse has an outstanding chance then you may offer the same advice the late Richard Baerlein gave his *Guardian* readers before Shergar's Derby: 'Now is the time to *bet like men*.'

Manger: 'He absolutely *licked out* his *manger* the night after the race.' It is a sign of a horse's *well-being*

that he is a *good doer* and *eats up well*, so a standard
way of saying a horse does not *know he has been in a
race* is to report the information that he has *eaten up*
afterwards. Trainers therefore attach particular
importance to inspecting the *manger* in each
inmate's box on their morning rounds: 'She had to
do it the *hard way* yesterday but I was delighted to see
her *manger* spotlessly clean.' There are several alternative words available, depending also on where in
the world the yard is located: 'He does everything you
ask and dives into his *trough* straight after racing';
'There was not a stalk left in his *cot* when we
checked'; 'He's put back 10kg in a day and *licked out*
his *feedbin* on Monday night.'

Manner: 'The *manner* of his victory here told us he
was **crying** *out* for another furlong's **trip**.' The example suggests that the *manner* of a horse's running
reflects a single, usually *eyecatching*, performance
whereas the *style* of a horse's racing takes account of
a whole career.

Manners: 'It was the second time Nevis had shown
wayward *manners* on the racetrack after winning her
first start at Kembla, and she has now been threatened with a ban by the stewards if she does not *mend
her ways*.' Although it is one of very few sports where
competitors of either gender can take part in the same
contest, racing has always had a chauvinistic side to
it, which sometimes extends to the horses as well as
the people. Perhaps it is our imagination, but fillies
and mares seem to be required by pundits and **horsemen** to mind their racecourse or stable *manners* more
than colts. Perhaps this is because *mareish* behaviour,
which ranges from *flashing* the tail to being a *right
madam* when **in season**, is perceived to be something
of a nightmare. However, scoldings about racecourse
etiquette are not entirely restricted to the dam side:

'Gelded during the winter, Albinus *disgraced himself* when refusing to enter the stalls at Newbury.'

Match: You never talk about a *match* in racing unless you are referring to a race that has ***cut up*** to only two runners or, more predictably, a race where you think only two runners have a chance: 'The opener amounts to a *match* between the Williams and Nicholls runners'; 'Probably a "*match race*", with Fastnet Rock and Alinghi resuming rivalry in Saturday's T. J. Smith Stakes at Randwick.' Any other usage is likely to be a reflection of other sports, as in this explanation given to excuse a horse's ***sketchy*** jumping: 'Shaadiva was as good as these over hurdles but lacked *match practice* over fences in what was a soundly run race.'

Match strides: Routinely, horses are said to *match strides* when *disputing the lead*, even if the two horses so described have very different ***actions***. We have heard Simon Holt notch up the idea by describing early leaders as *trading punches*, which is more innovative, and about as imaginative, as their *locking horns*.

Mid-div: Jockeys sometimes seem to carry their preoccupation with reducing weight into their vocabulary, where 'position' slims down to *posi* and *mid-division* sheds a couple of syllables to become *mid-div* (though the latter perhaps stems from this abbreviation in race-reading). The latter term can also have jurisdiction beyond races themselves, usually to mean ***moderate***: 'He's been in the *mid-div* of West Country trainers for some time.'

Mile: Tends to be the unit of measure for how far in front of a fence an extravagant jumper takes off – 'He *stood off* a *mile* at that ditch' – or for how far out of a race the stragglers are: 'Forget the rest – they're *miles* behind.' A *country mile* of course means a very long way: 'If Murphy's Cardinal is in the first three, and not beaten a *country mile*, he's likely to run at Cheltenham.' In the same style a horse might be described as finishing *several counties* behind the field. Meanwhile, with one of those regular metaphors that treat horses as cars, connections can talk of their horse having not many or too many *miles on the clock*.

Minesweeping: On the *exchanges*, the equivalent of finishing everybody else's drinks at a party is to lay a horse *in running* at any possible price, a practice which may make you equally sick if the horse then proceeds to *fly home* from an impossible position: 'Some traders were *minesweeping* the favourite but were left head in hands once he got back on the bridle.'

Mix it: In other words, to *join battle* up front rather than be **dropped out**: 'The Kew Tour was always *mixing it* in the first four.' The phrase can also bear on the campaign of a horse running in *hot **company***: 'Billy Vodan has been *mixing it* with some pretty decent stuff'; 'Divine Proportions has the profile of a top-class filly capable of *mixing it* with the colts.'

Moderate: The language of the racecard is spare, telegrammatic. Its readers need quickly to come to conclusions. The often dispassionate tone may be attributable to the fact that horses (apart from any Houyhnhnms visiting from *Gulliver's Travels*) will not be put out by withering comments such as the lapidary 'of little *account*'. Connections can take more offence. But that very common euphemism for **effing** useless – *moderate* – seems somehow crueller still for being temperate: 'Even by selling standards, these are a very *moderate* bunch and it is hard to find a winner.'

Money: While a selection of euphemisms may camouflage the fundamental purpose of the racing industry, you are allowed to be quite unequivocal about what is going on in the ring. 'The *money* is *down*' is the brisk way to say that connections *fancy* a horse and have backed it. Some trainers already have a smart reputation for pulling off a *coup*: 'Alan Swinbank rarely leaves the *money behind*.'

Monkey: More affectionate than calling an animal a *jade* or *rogue*, this sobriquet should be levelled primarily at those who are *characters* at best and **squiggle horses** at worst: 'Serov is some *monkey* but he likes it here at the Curragh.' A *monkey* in the ring is £500.

Monster: 'French Holly may have **blundered** his way to victory in this race but he was a *monster* whereas No Refuge is little bigger than a **pony**.' The noun *monster* clings to big horses, especially when they are awesome *gallopers*, and does not necessarily imply anything monstrous. The verb, on the other hand, would suggest a horse whose behaviour is *savage*: 'Emancipation used to *monster* Grahame Begg when he handled her for the family stable.' More regularly, though, *monster* features virtually as a synonym for **machine** or **tank**, as in this characteristic piece of training-yard discourse from Tom Foley: 'Royal Paradise will never *show* you at home how good he is. He'd make it hard work to *pull a donkey*. But he is a *monster* on the racecourse.'

More letters than numbers: 'He's got *more letters than numbers* this year and it's hard to see him playing a part in the finish.' These words could greet an uneven performance on *Countdown*, but here they offer an economic way of disparaging a horse, usually a jumper (of sorts) unless he is extremely accident-prone on the flat. All letters in the form printed by a runner's name on the racecard indicate a failure to *complete*, other than D (Disqualified) and V (Void), which indicate a failure to **collect**.

Motionless: 'Be Be King scored as he wanted in the *bumper* with Joe Tizzard sitting *motionless.*' The term immediately informs readers that the horse won without coming off the bridle. Such *armchair rides* are even easier than *steering jobs*. The implication will be picked up in live commentary also, as in: '*Here comes* Well Chief, with Timmy Murphy still sitting *motionless.*' It is much less good news if a jockey is seen *lying motionless*.

Mud: *Soft* and *heavy* are usually the official terminology but commentators seem to enjoy handling an honest word like *mud*, especially when there is a horse who seems to *relish* it: 'Yahoo loves it when the *mud's flying* like today'; 'Observer Corps is a real *mudlark* and won't like the prevailing good ground.' Horses that *flounder* in the mud are noted, but without any ado: 'Autcaesarautnihil got *stuck in the mud* at Leicester last week.' Never say 'muddy' going in Britain, although talk of a *muddy track* – and horses who like them as *mudders* – seems to be countenanced whenever dirt tracks are so wet they cannot be harrowed. See also *sloppy*.

Muddling: 'With several front runners in the field the Red Rum Handicap was never going to turn into a *muddling affair.*' If you cannot bring yourself to dignify a slow race by calling it *tactical*, this is your adjective.

Mug: Definitive for 'loser': 'In retrospect that was a real *mug's* bet on the Pipe horse when you see how well Remittance Man jumps.' We all like to think that everybody else is a *mug-punter*, even if we know racing can be a *mug's game*. In racing the *mug* is an unfulfilled version of the *face*.

Mulish: *Mules* get a consistently bad press in racing owing to the assumption that these animals never

want to *go a **yard***: 'She proved *mulish* in the stalls
and may have been ***in season***'; 'It was a most unchar-
acteristic and *mulish* display from Sabin du Loir, who
tried to ***plant*** himself and never seemed happy.' A
reference to *mulish behaviour* therefore invariably
indicates recalcitrance; if you just want to say a horse
is slow you would call him a *packhorse*, not a mule.

N

Nag: *Nag* once meant 'a small horse', but nowadays it
will typically be one that has lost you money: 'The
nag only went and got ***beat***.' Racing fans can also be
described as people who *follow* the *nags* or who ***play***
the ***gee-gees***, but not by other racing fans.

Nail: There are two situations in which jockeys and
their horses want to *nail* things. The first involves
measuring a fence perfectly, as in: 'He *nailed* the
last and the result was never then in doubt.' The
second requires catching the leader in the *shadow of
the post*: 'Promising 7 lb conditional Lee Stephens
nailed Ruby Walsh on the line to win the opener.'
This last example might sound painful, but only if
the metaphor really had any life in it. *Nailed on*, as a
standard way of describing a horse who is a good
thing, has also lost any distinct sense of its origins at
the forge.

Nanny goat: A taste for trimming words (like ***mid-
div***) is not confined to jockeys. The *Totalisator Board*
was always going to be contracted to *Tote*, and the
rhyming-slang version is itself sometimes abbreviated
to *Nanny*. The Tote comes into its own when you're
backing outsiders each way in very liquid *pools* or

if you are new to gambling and require assistance from the *ladies in red* – plus its profits, as it does not tire of telling us, *go back into racing*. However, the *Nanny* is disdained by some professional punters, who think it is for *suits* and *mugs*. In one memorable exchange on a late-night chat show Barney Curley told a man confessing his addiction to gambling: 'You must have a real problem if you're betting on the Tote, pal.'

Nap: The universal word for a tipster's strongest recommendation of the day, it often appears in brackets after the name of the selection (like *Nb*, which indicates the *next best* tip). The verb is also useful on a day-to-day basis: 'I *napped* him last time out at Windsor and believe he can *supplement gains* today.' Very occasionally a trainer with horses entered or declared in a race will be described as *nap-handed*: if he happens to have five runners the word is being used with historical correctness, in that the derivation is the card game *Napoleon*, where *going nap* meant you had won all five tricks.

Neck muscles: When a jockey has a *steering job* and looks around for *non-existent* dangers, the commentator may try to get a laugh by saying: 'The only muscles Dean is having to move to win this one are his *neck muscles*.' Marginally funnier if you've backed Dean's mount.

Nestle: In big handicaps, tipsters often find horses with *good racing weights* smuggled away at the bottom of the list, sometimes even when they *languish* out of the handicap: 'Monkerhostin jumps off the page *nestling* at the foot of the weights in the Paddy Power Gold Cup.' This statement seems awkward, if not paradoxical, but fortunately 'jumps off the page' is not a racing expression.

Never: If a horse runs *too bad to be true*, so that even the euphemism ***disappointing*** would be straining things, you can forgive jockeys for taking a little licence in explaining that they were *never* happy. So you will hear 'He *never* went a ***yard***' when the horse has been pulled up after two miles; or 'She *never* jumped a ***fence*** today' after the horse has completed in her own time despite numerous mistakes; or 'He was *never* ***travelling*** at all' when the horse seemed to be on the bridle for the first six furlongs. But in each case you know what the jockey means. As tends to happen with expressions in common parlance, the phrase '*never* at the races' is not said very often by racing people, although it can be heard if a horse has failed to give his *running*.

Never-nearer: Means what it says, but can have very different implications depending on the context. Thus, there are two possible inferences to be drawn from the report that 'Waydale Hill was a *never-nearer* sixth at Hexham'. The horse could have been running on at the death under ***tender*** handling, and therefore may be of *interest* next time out. Alternatively, he looked like a *slow* ***boat*** destined to be making up the numbers for the rest of his career. Trainers are adept at telling owners that *never-nearer* efforts should be interpreted in the former light.

Nick: Some jockeys are expert at *nicking* a few lengths at the start, and trainers always like to have their string in *good nick*, but the most specialised usage is in breeding: a *blood nick* occurs when two unrelated families consistently produce a successful outcome.

Niggle: Takes the prepositions *at* and *along*: 'Aixparu was *niggling at* the mare from a long way out'; 'Charm Offensive responded to being *niggled along*.'

Reserved to describe how a jockey rides a lazy horse who has to be *kept up* to his *work* from early in a race rather than the more frantic *scrubbing along* that can occur at the *business end*.

Nobble: The classic verb for those situations where a horse has been interfered with: 'Milk It Mick has been *nobbled*.' The alternative phrase *got at* seems to envisage phalanxes of racecourse security which the would-be race-fixer must penetrate, whereas history seems to show that it is relatively easy to drug or otherwise interfere with a racehorse if you really want to. That said, it is probably safe to say that the *form book* is unlikely to contain future entries like the one Zoedene received in the 1885 National: 'Fell, *poisoned*.'

Nose: In America, a *nose* is the shortest possible winning distance. Although the official equivalent in Britain and Ireland is a *short head*, it is possible to improvise in describing a particularly close call. Hence: 'One late lunge got Vista Bella home by a *nostril*,' or François Doumen's comment on the 1991 Gold Cup where The Fellow 'just failed, by the width of a *Gauloise* paper, to reach Garrison Savannah'. This surely deserves to be adopted as an official measure. *On the nose* is a colloquialism for a bet on the win rather than each way, presumably driven by the fact that your selection will have to get its *nose* in front of all the other horses. See also *eat the turf*.

Not a bother: Felicitous Irish phrase to emphasise nothing at all is *amiss* with a horse: 'Baracouda's fine and there's *not a bother* on him, but the trainer's decided to go straight to Cheltenham without another run.' Humans involved in the *game* can be blessed likewise: 'Walsh's *agent*, sister Jennifer, said after his fall: "He's fine – sore but otherwise there's *not a bother* on him".'

Notebooks: These lend themselves to a ritualised way of recording an *eyecatching* victory: 'Chelsea Bridge went into *many people's notebooks* after getting the better of Trabolgan at Kempton.' Potentially as useful as the old binoculars for serious punters.

Nothing: What *bridle* horses *find* when they come under pressure: 'Quicks The Word *found nothing* when *given the office*.' Abbreviated in race-reading to '*found nil*'.

Not knocked about: 'Best Mate was *not knocked about* once his *chance had gone*.' This is a more or less neutral way of saying that use of the whip has come to an end. The negative is obligatory, so that you would not think of saying: 'Culloty knocked Best Mate about mercilessly once the horse was headed.' Nevertheless, while the jockey in the race, to *accept the situation*, eventually goes easy, the phrase itself might be seen as an indirect admission that horses do not *come out* of *hard races* well. In the same way, commentators are happy to observe that a horse firmly *made use of* was not subjected to *undue punishment*, but are much less likely to draw attention to any over-committed acts of *persuasion*.

Not off: A sinister expression. It does not mean 'false start' but that one particular runner is not *trying* (*not meant* is a rarer alternative).

Not seen out: 'African Dream was *not seen out* again after finishing 7th of 12 in a Group 3 at Salisbury.' It sounds like poor African Dream was (and perhaps deserved to be) *confined* to his box, whereas he has merely not appeared on a racecourse since. During a race a commentator is more likely to say that a horse has not been *sighted* (meaning that, though visible, he was not very near the front). Alternatively, if the commentator cannot be bothered to summon a *search party*, he may settle for a merciless: 'Never *called* him. Never *saw* him.'

Novicey: 'He was a bit *novicey* early on but got the hang of things on the second circuit.' Novice hurdlers and chasers, being in their first season over those obstacles (or their eighth if they are too *moderate* ever to lose their *maiden* tag), are forgiven some of their clumsiness at their fences with what is itself a rather clumsily contrived adjective. But then racing seems to have a predilection for adopting words on this model, to judge by *scopey, rangey, gluey, Oaksey*.

Nowhere: 'Eclipse first, the rest *nowhere*': these famous words, emphatic as they are simple, first uttered by an oracular punter at Ascot in 1770, still resonate in rather lower grades: 'Miss Academy first, the rest *nowhere* – that's the simple analysis of this modest contest.' In the era of Eclipse, *nowhere* indicated the *distance* behind at which you were disqualified, whereas these days you are allowed to *finish nowhere* if you wish to *continue*.

Nudge: 'Lowestoft Playboy just being *nudged along* now.' The verb possibly denotes those initial attentions to a horse as it comes off the bridle. A jockey will, with increasing urgency, *nudge along, squeeze along, niggle along, shuffle along* and *row away*. By then the whip will be *up*, if he has not administered *reminders* already.

Nut: Colloquialism for *head* seen in such phrases as: 'He was done a *short nut* at Sandown,' or 'He's the sort of horse who really gets his *nut* down.' A common expression, no easier to explain than *game as a pebble*, sees horses *travelling* as *sweet as a nut*.

O

Off: Turns into a noun to indicate the start of a race: 'From the *off*, Keen Leader looked unhappy on the ground'; 'Theatre was as long as 11/4 in *places* by the *off*.' But the preposition is already a favoured one in a number of racing situations: 'The horse is always best coming *off of* a fast pace'; '*Off* a nice weight of 8-8, Moonshine Bill may have a better chance than *bounce* theorists suggest'; 'High Fly comes into the Florida Derby *off of* a victory in the Fountain of Youth Stakes.' Note also that for horses, as for most batsmen and (we hope) all motorists, the *off side* is the right-hand side: 'He's got a little cut on his *off* fore.'

Off-course: The distinction between *on-course* and *off-course* is largely relevant to cash bookmakers – particularly so when it is illegal for them to operate *off-course* (as it was in Britain between 1853 and 1961) or when a different rate of *Ajax* applies depending on whether you have *come racing* or not. But should you hear the phrase *off-track*, this is an American expression, innocent of anything to do with betting or tax, for *give* in the ground: 'Kitten's Joy likes it kind of *off-track* as we say in the States, so if it's *yielding* or *soft* at Longchamp that will suit him just fine.' In this example, the connections' *sporting* attitude has not extended to their learning the French terms *collant* and *souple*.

Office: When jockeys *give* their horses *the office*, they are not expecting to have their photocopying done but are asking their mounts to *go on* at the *business end* of a race: 'Once Sean's *given* him *the office*, he's *picked up* nicely.' If this usage derives from 'offering the sacrament', we are inclined to gloss it as more Irish than

Catholic in its adoptive context. '*Office* money' is a term seen at the end of lists of big individual bets in the on-course ring: there is perhaps a suggestion, even more sniffy in the age of the *exchanges*, that *high-street* punters never bet large.

Old: Racehorses command loyalties which, transcending the transitory alliance of backer and backed, are registered in the way racegoers welcome *old friends* who reappear season after season, even if they eventually become *friendless* in the betting market. So when Peter O'Sullevan talks about '*old man* Galmoy', he is being affectionate not ageist, while references to *old soldiers* or *old warriors* do not mean that there is a collection box on the way round. Flat horses too, like Persian Punch, can be acknowledged as *old hands* or *old stagers* in the nicest possible sense. Mind you, *old rogues* or **monkeys** are not quite so lovable (nor necessarily so *old*): 'He's **dogged it** today and is becoming a bit of an *old rogue*.'

Omit: Whenever a hurdle or fence is **dolled off** on the first circuit or is not jumped at all (perhaps owing to the state of the ground or even a low winter sun), it is invariably *omitted* – perhaps because horses who *miss one out* have just as invariably *stepped right through* an obstacle without taking off.

On: A little word with some important meanings for racing people. In the common phrase 'He's still very much on it,' *it* refers to the *bridle*. When a *paddock judge* says, 'There's a little bit left *on* her,' this means the filly he is looking at is carrying a little **condition**. Commentators will also remark whether there is any pace *on* early in a race, or look out for horses that might be keen to *go on*. It is of course the standard preposition for gamblers – 'Who are you *on* in the Coronation Cup ?' – as if to suggest that they are **up**

there with the jockeys when betting. And indeed money itself will also duly *ride on* the outcome.

On board: A regular synonym for *up*, as in 'Frenchman's Creek looks interesting again with Paul Carberry *on board*.' The jockey is in no danger of being recorded as 'overboard', but he is quite liable to be *unshipped*. But a rider will be credited with keeping the *partnership afloat* even when it is the horse who has done well to *find a leg*.

One pace: Any horse without a *turn of foot* is, sadly, *one-paced*. So this word is inevitably pejorative, however qualified: 'He's as honest as the day is long but I suppose in Listed *company* he is a little bit *one-paced*.' One of the commonest phrases in potted race-reading is of the kind *'one pace* from two out'. This is instantly comprehensible to punters as meaning 'He kept going but not any quicker'; or, to use the race-reading jargon again, the horse did not *weaken* but he did not *stay on* either. Note that flat-race-reading, perhaps recognising that horses tend to have more *gears* on the level, tends to prefer other summary terms like *no extra* or *not quicken* rather than *one pace*. Race-reporting often brings in the definite article before *one pace*, which has the effect of making the prose *plod on* as slowly as the horse: 'After *menacing* around the home turn, The Spoonplayer could only *run on* at *the one pace* in the straight.' Not to be confused with *on-pace*, which is the Australian for a horse who races *handy*: 'Garrison Savannah's an *on-pace* runner and Darren Beadman should be able to get him *over* from barrier 7.'

On his tod: A singular case of an expression that has gone into the language but has lapsed in racing, where it originated. J. F. 'Tod' Sloan, the American jockey given to running races in England from the front, was always 'out on his own' – hence, with the rhyming surname discarded, *on his Tod*. Perhaps some *acey-deucy* was involved.

On sufferance: An affable way of referring to the situation where one horse is in close proximity with another but only because the latter is toying with or, more pointedly, *laughing* at him: 'Armaturk followed in close attendance but was only there *on sufferance.*'

Order: This word looks to have acquired a slightly more professional cachet than *form* or *nick*: 'He's in very good *order*'; 'I've never had him in better *order.*' In a different usage, runners who have been dropped out early can take *closer order* as the race develops. See also *under starter's orders*.

Organise: 'He's some young rider. Did you see the way he was *organising* the horse at his fences?' To *organise* is therefore to *present*, but with the likely distinction that, whereas *presenting* a horse at his obstacles seems to suggest an effortless rhythm, *organising* him allows for the possibility that he is the type of animal who needs his *mind made up* for him. This still leaves some residual responsibility with the horse for getting his stride pattern worked out: 'The low sun made it very difficult for him to meet the fences right and *organise* himself.'

Out-and-out: The most popular adjective for a *stayer*, just ahead of *dour* and *thorough*.

Out like a light: 'Green Star *disappointed* when going *out like a light* at Market Rasen and *trailing in* over 22 lengths seventh.' The formula here is certainly definitive enough to describe the fairly common phenomenon of a horse who goes from having every

chance to *treading water* in a *matter of strides*.
Interchangeable with *stopped as if shot*.

Outpointed: A synonym for *beat* in race reports:
'Elle Roseador came up the stand rail to *outpoint*
Ballyhoo'; 'Little Big Horse had *every chance* at the
second last but was *readily outpointed.*' Taken straight
from boxing, and so not altogether apposite in racing, where going the distance speaks for itself. Still
effective, though, as a way of recording an emphatic
victory, as in this variation: 'My Will was beaten
pointless over two miles on this course in November.'

Over the top: In racing at least, nothing to do with
World War I. Used when a horse is no longer showing
progressive form and is proved to have had at least *one
race too many*: 'We thought we'd get away with it
today but he's run a *shocker* and looks like he's *over
the top* for the season'; 'Kings Quay's form *tailed off*
last season but I think he was *over the top.*' See also *go
to the well*.

Owe: It is natural for racing people to attribute to
horses the same moral qualities that are recognised in
human life. The soldiering tradition lives on in com-
mendations of *equine* bravery and gallantry. If *old
soldiers* never die, all the more reason to look forward
to their superannuation: 'He doesn't *owe* anybody
anything and we will retire him as soon as he *tells us*
he's not *enjoying* it.'

P

Pack: The image of the *chasing pack* is often invoked
by commentators, against the grain of evolution,

since horses are flight animals. *Peleton* is uttered in its season by those race-callers who have been watching the Tour de France on television. Then, in an astute readaptation of the metaphor, horses who come *fast and late* to win can *trump* the *pack*.

Paddle: 'Oops, the leader really *paddled* his way through that one.' When a horse cannot *see a stride*, the action of his front legs as he tries to clear a fence conjures up this image.

Paddock: *Paddock watcher* or *paddock judge* are the collective names for those specialists who base their judgements primarily on how a horse looks in the parade ring rather than how he reads in the *form book*. They are signed up to identify the *pick of the paddock* for television viewers. But in the plural, *paddocks* are the places to which racehorses, especially mares who will become *brood mares*, head off when they retire from racing to make a *visit* or two.

Parish: Horses that arrive with a late burst from nowhere are often said to come from *another parish*. The lateness is the trigger for this image, which evokes the atavistic memory of a stand-in curate rushing across the fields, and conceivably jumping the hedges, in order to arrive *distressed*, but just in time to start the service. The usage would then seem to be designed for *steeplechasers* but is by no means confined to them. Perhaps the ecclesiastical reference is a little ironic, given the suspicion with which the sport has sometimes been regarded from pulpits, or maybe it testifies to the essentially parochial nature of racing itself. Paul Hayward may agree with the second explanation, as he once wrote eloquently about the way Desert Orchid, like Arkle before him, 'built up a following outside racing's narrow *parish*'.

Part company: An *unseated* may sound less embarrassing and even rather gracious when described in the following terms: 'Steve Smith Eccles *parted company* with Southernair at that one.' *Came unstuck* seems quite literally more down-to-earth.

Partner: 'Johnny Murtagh will *partner* Soviet Song again in the Sussex Stakes.' A rider will typically and unobtrusively be said to *partner* his horse (and over jumps the *partnership* will be said to remain *intact* if they nearly fall). It is a neat tribute to the symbiosis of *man and **beast*** essential to racing success, but note that the jockey is always the subject and the horse the object in sentences featuring the equitable verb.

Passage: The noun to describe the progress of a ***holdup horse*** through the field. Sometimes a jockey will negotiate a *clear passage*, sometimes he is less skilful or lucky and gets a *bumpier* ride: 'I went right down the *inner* and got a great *passage*'; 'Arakan endured a *nightmare passage* when runner-up to Nayyir in the Lennox.'

Peach: Before a race, a jockey (or his ***agent***) is said to have secured a *plum ride*. After it, he may look back upon a *peach of a ride* – virtually any winning ride can be so described, even if you made a complete ***horlicks*** of the tactics. Obviously, plums are especially mouthwatering while peaches are altogether delicious.

Pegasus: The classical allusion is unsleeved for a very fast-finishing horse, whose *chance* appeared to *have gone*, but who is suddenly able to accelerate past the other finishers: 'Frenchman's Creek *finished like Pegasus* up the Cheltenham hill.' Those with no Greek might have offered less erudite versions like 'Frenchman's Creek *sprouted wings*,' or 'Frenchman's

Creek *came from the clouds.*' The first metaphor is even
more common in live commentary as the favourite's
chance is slipping away: 'He's *responding* to the whip
but he'll have to *sprout wings* to win from there.'

Penny: Used either of *green* two-year-olds or novice
jumpers: 'The *penny* is only dropping with him now
but he's getting the hang of hurdles and will make a
lovely chaser one day.' The expression can also be
used in running when a horse takes some time to get
the message from his jockey: 'Murphy had administered stern **reminders** to Field Roller but the *penny*
finally *dropped* in the home straight.' In Australia, it
seems you can ask your horse to *find* acceleration off
the bridle measured in units of currency even smaller
than *ten bob*: 'When they got to the 300 metre mark I
could see Nash hadn't *asked a penny* of Elvstroem and
was just going to go away.'

Percentage: Racing's way of saying that a jockey is
legitimately entitled to count his chickens: 'Norman
Williamson has time to *work out his percentage* as
Teeton Mill **sluices** home.' Jockeys receive a *percentage* of win and place prize money, which gives rise to
this knowing way of calling an easy winner home,
especially in a race with a big *pot*.

Persuader: Rather a hackneyed term for the jockey's
whip, but it is a staple of commentary when a horse
is receiving considerable **assistance**, as in these two
examples heard within an hour of each other on different sides of the Irish Sea: 'Dix Villez's jockey has
now *resorted* to the *persuader*'; 'Indien Royal is feeling
the *warmth* of Christian Williams's *persuader.*' The
euphemism can look a little more quaint in written
journalism, but it occasionally appears: 'As usual
Murphy had to get the *persuader* out on Stormez, but
the horse *responded* well *for* **pressure.**'

Pick off: Means to 'go past' a series of runners, with the implication that if they have been *shot* down they will not go back past you. The usage applies most naturally to a victory by a ***hold-up horse*** or *closer*: 'Giacomo came from an unpromising position turning into the stretch to *pick off* his rivals one by one.' But it can also work for a more run-of-the-mill performance: 'He *picked a few off* in the straight but was basically just *running through* tired horses.'

Pick of grass: Horses in training, on the sort of high-protein diet that may turn them a little ***fizzy***, are often given a break in their regime by being allowed out for what is invariably called a *pick of grass*. This can also seem to prove a horse's well-being after a race, whether or not he has *licked out* his ***manger***: 'He had a hard race but went out for a *pick of grass* this morning and seems as right as rain.'

Pick up: 'She was ***travelling*** sweetly but just didn't *pick up* for me when I *let* her *down*'; 'With Baron Windrush we will ***drop*** him *in* and then *pick up.*' These clusterings of phrasal verbs can become confusing, but whether it is the horse or the jockey doing the *picking up*, the idea is that they should be accelerating in the closing stages. *Pick up* can also be used to mean ***pick off***: 'He *picked up* the leader in a *matter of strides* when *given* the ***office.*'

Pilot error: 'He shot clear of a big field but *pilot error* lost him the race as he was eased to a walk at the last and could not ***pick up*** again.' Just as aircraft manufacturers will find some relief if an enquiry into a fatal accident arrives at this explanation, so connections, especially if they lose the race in a *stewards' enquiry*, find that blaming the jockey is the easiest way of convincing themselves that their horse's ***engine*** is yet in perfect working order.

Ping: To jump a fence really well, and so gain rather than lose momentum: 'He's really *pinged* the last and they were never going to get to him after that.' Seems to belong with *wing* and *zing* in a more or less onomatopoeic series of verbs for launching at fences.

Pinhooking: Bloodstock term for buying foals and selling them on as yearlings. This activity has the potential to be economically sensible for two reasons: the stock (the *pinhook*) is purchased after the trials and expenses of breeding the foal have been borne by somebody else, and then sold before any racecourse appearances have had the chance to give the lie to the animal's pedigree: 'It is the *pinhookers' game* to buy cheap and sell high, and an individual who has developed well and *breezes* exceptionally can easily leave a modest yearling price behind.' Not to be confused with *pinsticking*, which *housewives* were supposed to do once a year for the Grand National.

Pipe opener: Following the well-tested view that horses need a *blow* to get themselves *spot on*, trainers will often describe a *prep race*, where they are not necessarily aiming to win but to *blow away* the *cobwebs*, as a *pipe opener*. The phrase can also apply to a fast piece of work done at home to *set up* a horse for a particular target. Journalists sometimes find it hard to resist a punning headline if the first race at the meeting they are covering is won by a certain trainer from Nicholashayne.

Pitch: 'Mubtaker going best but Dubai Success is still *in there pitching*.' This is what the commentator will tend to say when one horse is not *travelling* quite as well as another but is still laying down a challenge. The metaphor comes from baseball and implies that the horse in question does not yet need to be 'relieved' by another pitcher, but there might also be a suggestion here that Dubai Success is not on as *even a keel* as Mubtaker.

Place: The verb identifies what many people believe to be a trainer's most important skill – namely, finding races in the ***programme book*** whose conditions will particularly suit his horse or which might ***cut*** up to only a few runners: 'Philip Hobbs is a master of *placing* his handicappers to *best advantage*.' Occasionally, if the race has turned out much more difficult than expected, or the winning trainer has had outrageous luck with non-runners or fallers, the phrase can be used with irony: 'Let's just say that was brilliantly *placed*, shall we?' *In places* is used in betting reports to mean a price was available at some but not all *pitches*; *in a place* means one bookmaker was brave or foolish enough to offer an outlying price, which was probably *snapped up* in seconds by the pros.

Planted: Horses can literally *dig* their *heels in*, which is particularly noteworthy if this means they do not *consent* to start: 'She's *planted* herself in front of the stalls and look *most reluctant* to take part'; 'I don't know what else Tony was supposed to do as Deano's Beeno was completely *planted*.'

Plate: On the assumption that the prize for lower-grade races will be a *plate* not a cup (sometimes ***gaff tracks*** struggle to muster up a second-hand picture frame), this is the metonym for *selling* class: 'He's only a *plater* so his ***proximity*** to the winner devalues the form'; 'She's won in *plating **company*** before so can't be opposed here.' *Plate* can also be a synonym for saddle, particularly when you remain in it after a ***blunder***: 'Tom Doyle did well to *stay* in the *plate* there.' Most punters are also aware that *spread a plate* is the technical term for a racehorse losing a shoe, because whenever they hear these words during the

preliminaries they know there will be a delay –
particularly if the farrier has to be located in one of
the racecourse bars and then has to run down to the
starting area putting up a few pounds overweight.

Play: This verb casts the jockey in the role of a card
sharp who knows just when to show his hand: 'John
Francome *played* Sea Pigeon *very late* to deny
Pollardstown and Daring Run.' But the word is also
encountered as a synonym for 'bet on': 'I've *played*
Pico Central in the Shaheen.' Possibly this is a reflection of French connections translating the word *jouer*,
but it tallies more explicitly with the way Americans
can refer to punters: 'Those *credentials* led *horseplayers* around the globe to make the colt the 7/2
favorite in the Breeders' Cup Mile.'

Play up: The verb chides the horse usually before the
start of a race, and very often in the stalls: 'This isn't
the first time he's *played up* after being loaded.'
Perhaps in these circumstances a euphemism for 'rear
up'. There are other confined spaces which horses
can baulk at: 'Chorist was being loaded on a plane to
France for the Prix de l'Opéra when she *played up*
and banged her head, resulting in her withdrawal.'

Plenty: Ubiquitous in racing parlance: 'He found
plenty'; 'It's *plenty* soft enough for him'; 'There
are *plenty of opportunities* for a horse of his type';
'*Plenty* in with a chance as they hit the three-pole';
'Intrigued has *plenty going* for her.'

Plot: *Plot one up* is the canonical expression for the
calculated attempt to keep a horse *unexposed* prior to
unleashing him in a big handicap: 'I fear the prize
money for the Fred Winter compared to the Triumph
will encourage the wily and crafty to *plot one up* for
the handicap'; 'Unless Martin Pipe has *plotted up* a

seasonal debutant, look to those with a recent run against their name.'

Plough through: The operative verb when a horse *flattens* or upsets a hurdle, sometimes testimony to that horse's tenacity in going on unchecked but, as often, a suitably agricultural tribute to the stolid animal's inability to jump.

Plunge: One of the main figures of speech for a concerted gamble: 'Morris was **on board** Mr Midland for the O'Grady team, landing a massive *plunge* in the National Hunt Chase.' A nice image which conjures up the ideas of the plummeting price on offer, and the punters *falling over themselves* to **get** *on*. It has been current since the nineteenth century (the Victorian punter E. H. Benson was known as the *Jubilee Plunger*) but, in the age of Betfair, *plunges* seem to be more easily reversible: 'It is always a difficult call as to whether to back these *ante-post plunges* these days, because all those on at **big** prices will be laying off this morning on the *exchanges*.'

Pogo-stick jump: Infrequently used term for the way in which certain horses who are not the most *natural* of jumpers *negotiate* the obstacles. But effective in conveying the sense that the horse has achieved vertical lift-off with inadequate forward propulsion: 'He's been *good* up to now but that was the first rather *pogo-stick jump* from Carvill's Hill today.'

Pony: A bet of £25. But also denoting a horse who could not be said to have **scope**: 'Linus O'Reilly is little more than a *pony* but he certainly has a big heart.' And if that's not contemptuous enough: '"Look at that one over there," Nigel says, pointing to another runner in the paddock. "*My Little Pony*, that is".'

Pop: 'He *popped* the first and *settled* really well'; 'The last circuit was a real pleasure *popping* away on him, knowing nothing was coming from behind.' This verb occurs in racing to suggest comfort in jumping, so that the clearance of obstacles sounds as routine as *popping* to the loo or the shops. *Popping* is certainly not as bold as *pinging*, which is why it tends to be seen in descriptions of schooling sessions where the emphasis is on not *spooking* the horse: 'We *popped* him over some tyres and he did it nicely.'

Preliminaries: These refer to the stretch of time from the moment a horse is *saddled up* to the moment of the *off*. The word is likely to be heard particularly when there is a *parade* for a big race. A horse can *ruin his chance* if he gets too *fizzy* or *worked up* during these procedures: 'Bachelor Duke managed only seventh at Ascot, *fighting for his head* under restraint for a long way after becoming *stirred up* in the *preliminaries*.' But there may still be time for a temperamental animal to recover composure after a decent amount of *playing up*: 'Valixir *flashed his tail* in the *prelims* but raced *kindly* up with the pace.'

Preparation: When horses are *laid out* for a particular race, it is often as if they are sitting an entrance exam: 'Ecomium is to be *prepared* by Jeremy Noseda for a *crack* at the Winter Derby on March 19.' The *preparation* can be *perfect*, but is more likely to be reported on if *not ideal* or *interrupted*: 'She's had a stone bruise and so her *preparation* has not been as we'd liked.' We have also seen the leading Australian trainer Gai Waterhouse use the word to mean the length of time a horse is in full training before being *spelled*: 'Grande Armee doesn't usually have more than six starts a *preparation*.'

Prepotent: 'Some sires like St Simon are *prepotent* and *stamp* their stock.' The ability of a sire to imbue his progeny with a disproportionate amount of his genetic characteristics is admirable, on the grounds that he will usually have been a much better racehorse than the mares he *covers*. Perhaps this is why the Polish word for *sire* is *reproduktor*. We were so impressed with the opening sentence here that we have learned it by heart and now use it for elocution practice.

Present: 'There was nobody better at *presenting* a horse at a fence than John Francome.' The verb encapsulates the skill of *seeing a **stride*** for your mount and making any necessary adjustments so that he can meet the jump perfectly. Compare ***organise***. Fences themselves can be described as *well presented* or *inviting*.

Press the button: This time the metaphor turns the horse into a rocket rather than a motor car, to describe the defining moment in a race when a jockey asks for sudden acceleration: 'When Joe *pressed the button*, I was pleased to see an immediate response.'

Pressure: *Under pressure* is perhaps the most frequently used opposite to *on the **bridle*** (even ahead of *off the **bridle***). *Coming under pressure* usually heralds the raising of the whip, but may, like *strong driving*, mean merely that the jockey is *rowing away*, with ***hands and heels***, for all he is worth. Notice the preposition used when a horse *responds* to such *urgings*: 'North Light ran on *for pressure* to come second.'

Primed: 'Perouse is reportedly *fully primed* for this good prize.' A perfectly acceptable metaphor for having a horse nicely ***wound up*** for his target. Perhaps not for the superstitious if it admits the possibility of ***blowing up***.

Principals: Suave term for *leaders*, whether in the *market* or in the race itself, though not as classy as *animateurs*, their French counterparts. Only to be found in the plural.

Problems: 'Plutocrat has had his share of *problems* but is useful on his day.' An example (compare **setback**) of how racing parlance can prefer more euphemistic terms for 'injury'. Common in the plural, as above, to mean that a horse is injury-prone.

Process: 'She was in the *process* of running a good race at Wolverhampton on her reappearance when she got a bit tired and started to **hang**.' Whenever you read about horses being in the *process* of running a *big race*, you know you are about to be told about them *going **out like a light***, falling over or otherwise not finishing as well as they started.

Procession: 'Grouse Moor *turned* the two-mile handicap hurdle *into a procession **under*** Leighton Aspell.' Winning connections may enjoy such situations, but the big bookmakers will always be ready to complain if racing becomes too *processional*.

Produce: A verb enlisted to praise either a trainer for bringing his horse to the race *spot on*, or, more commonly, a jockey for **pressing the button** at just the right moment (especially if the horse does not want to be *in front too soon*): 'The Beckett yard is developing a reputation for *producing* them at the first time of asking'; 'He came late but won nicely and Richard Quinn is brilliant at *producing* them like that.' A strong verb, in the sense that you know who's in charge.

Programme book: 'Legatus always seems to *bump* into *one too good* but given his trainer's *prowess* with the *programme book* he should be found a **little**

opportunity to get his **head in front**.' This does not
mean that his handler will be using the *programme
book* to assault the winners his horse keeps bumping
into, but that his encyclopaedic knowledge of the
fixtures and conditions will cure the **seconditis**.

Proximity: This is a dirty word in race-reading
when you are trying to weigh up whether the form of
a race *amounts* to anything: 'Her *proximity* in third
does not *advertise* the form particularly.' In other
words, a demonstrably bad horse getting within three
lengths of the **principals** suggests that the race was
falsely run or that the form does not *add up to much*
anyway. Whereas, when the leading pair in a race
have *drawn clear*, or when the proven **rags** are tailed
off *out the back*, the value of the race for future pre-
dictive purposes always seems to be rubber-stamped:
'They were soon *well strung out* so the form should
work out.' Indeed, there is a little parenthesis in previews which always means 'good form': 'Muqbil and
Vespone meet again after their battle royal at
Newbury (*pair clear*).'

Pull: One of racing's key words, relating to the taut-
ness of the reins, where it makes a great difference
whether the horse or the jockey is doing the *pulling*.
Horses who are a *bit* **keen** are known to *pull hard* or
pull like a train or *pull for their head* (or can simply be
called *strong pullers*). In a race, if not under sufficient
restraint, these *headstrong* types will often *pull themselves* to the front or try to *pull the jockey's arms out*.
Often, the first time the rider gets involved in these
situations – over jumps at least – is when he has to
pull the horse *up* once his mount has *shot his bolt*.
Though note that, even here, if a horse has his *own
ideas about the **game***, he can be described as in control of his own exit from the race: 'And it looks as if
Parlezvousfrancais is trying to *pull himself up*.' A

much more positive action by a jockey is to *take a pull*. He can do this at any time in a race to slow his mount down, but the most dramatic effect is when he deliberately checks his progress in order not to get to the front *too soon*: 'Look how cheekily Graham Bradley continues to *take a pull* on Morley Street with the rest *hard at it.*' In these circumstances Bradley is *pulling double* (see also **double handful**), although this phrase can also be used in commentary just to mean that a horse is still going well. *Taking a pull* is such an established idea that it can be used metaphorically about a horse's training regime or a stable's activity: 'They were all **coughing** so badly that we just had to *take a pull* for the whole of January.' Finally,it is standard practice when discussing handicaps to talk about a *pull* in one horse's favour compared to the previous occasion he met an opponent: 'Right Approach has a seven-pound *pull* with Alkaadhem for a three-quarters-of-a-length beating last time over course and distance.'

Pull through: Rarely in service to praise a horse for winning tenaciously, but concerned rather with the action of a jockey when he transfers his whip from one hand to another, especially when his horse is *hanging*: 'He should have *pulled* his whip *through* to his left hand there and I would be surprised if there isn't an *objection.*'

Punch: Tired horses can occasionally be described as *punch-drunk*, but a reference to being *punched out* will not be to a chaser built like George Foreman exhausted by his efforts, but to a flat horse being *kept up* to his *work* with vigorous **hands and heels**: 'Aggravation, *punched out* by Steve Drowne, opens his account.' The jockey perhaps most associated with *punching out* horses without resorting to the whip was Willie Carson.

Push out: Usually a sign of a fairly easy victory, where the jockey has had only to *shake the reins* rather than get too *serious*: 'Mukddaam had only to be *pushed out* to score *readily*.' Bookmakers *push* a horse *out* in a different sense when they offer longer odds on it.

Put away: This is the standard verb when you *rough off* a horse, anticipating that he will go on to better things upon his return: 'Oscar Brunel will go for a novice hurdle somewhere and then we'll *put him away* for the season as chasing is his *game*.' Promising young horses, like vintage bottles of port, are sometimes difficult for trainers to *put away*, despite their best intentions. The expression may have reconciled Peter Shilton to the idea that his horses with Martin Pipe did not need to be fed over the summer, a delusion and a defence in court less likely in Australia, where horses are *put aside* in these circumstances.

Put down: There is an obviously sombre meaning (although racing prefers the expression *humanely destroyed*), but the primary usage is in the winter *game* when jockeys explain how their horse did not *see* the same *stride* as they did, and therefore *put in* another one rather than take off: 'I *asked* him for everything at the second last and when he *put down* on me there our chance was gone.'

Put it up: We have seen the expression *put it up* in Irish journalism, used in the same way as *serve it up*: 'Assuming he has improved from his first run of the season, Flagship Uberalles should *put it up* to the selection'; 'Two and a half out I thought Jack Sullivan was really going to *put it up* to them, but he just didn't *get* the *trip*.' The preposition appears to be variable if not to say volatile: 'It's been our target all sea-

son and I hope Rule Supreme can *put it down* to
Baracouda.'

Put to sleep: Another metaphor (compare *smuggle*)
for successfully restraining a *headstrong* animal is to
put him *to sleep*. Greville Starkey *put* Dancing Brave *to
sleep* right at the back of the field in the 1986 Derby,
only to complain that he 'couldn't wake the bugger up
again'.

Q

Quicken: Usually, but not always, accompanied by
the preposition *up*. The ability to *quicken*, especially
on the flat and especially *off* a fast pace is a prized
attribute. 'Not *quicken*' is race-reading shorthand for
a horse who can only run on at *the one pace* when
asked to **pick up**. While an ability to 'accelerate' is
validated by other sports, terse racing prose naturally
favours the quicker word.

Quiet: Sometimes used by the *Racing Post* to describe
a trainer's form, suggesting in a courteous way that
the yard might be *under a cloud*: 'Cherub can improve
and be a *major player* in this but the O'Neill yard has
been *a bit quiet* of late.' Consider also this sentence
from the aforesaid O'Neill about one of his stable
stars: 'Iris has been a bit *quiet* and worked *flat* so it's
best to take things *quietly* with him.' Here the adjective
means 'below par', the adverb 'easy'.

Quinella: A punter trying to put on four of these
dual forecast bets risks being **warned off** the track for
bad language, but they are popular where they are
available (in Argentina the bet is known, perhaps

inauspiciously, as an *imperfecta*). The **Nanny** has
borrowed the American word *exacta* for its *straight
forecasts*. It seems recommended that the names of
any *exotic wagers* should finish in *-ella*, *-ecta* or *-acta*.
A *superfecta* bet on the first four to be placed sounds
as if it has been around a long time, although if it was
available on chariot-racing in Roman times it might
have been called an *alia iacta*. Note that in Australia,
when a trainer is responsible for sending out horses
who fill the first three home, his achievement can
be reported as if he had placed a forecast bet on the
outcome himself (perhaps sometimes he does): 'A
stunned Guy Walter created Doncaster history when
he became the first trainer to claim the *trifecta* in the
Randwick showpiece with the least fancied of his
runners, Patezza, leading the trio.'

Quirks: The requisite term when talking about a
horse who has idiosyncrasies of character, but nothing
to stop him winning: 'He has his *quirks* but he's *genuine* enough when all is said and done.' **Kinks** and
kinky are respective synonyms and do not provide
jockeys with any excuse for extra use of the whip.

Quit the saddle: Like retiring footballers, jockeys
may *hang up their boots* when they've had enough. But
the preferred formula sees them *quit the saddle*. This
verb must be used since the alternatives risk giving
the impression that the jockey has simply fallen off.

R

Racing: The sport of kings seems to require no qualification: it simply is *racing*, without any need for a
prefix. Therefore all other forms of racing usually do

need an introduction, be it *drag, greyhound, motor*, or
– if you are a Nik Kershaw fan – *human racing.*

Racing weight: Has two meanings, one relating to the
amount of **condition** a horse is carrying – 'Azertyuiop's
preparation is being geared to Cheltenham and he is
above his optimum *racing weight*' – the other to a competitive mark in a handicap: 'Monte Cinto's got a nice
racing weight and I'm hoping for better.'

Rags: Means *rank* outsiders in the betting: 'It's 14/1
It Takes Time and then you're down to the *rags*';
'Beef Or Salmon never looked happy, trailing the field
as if one of the *rags.*' Derivation unknown but perhaps it arises when jockeys *cut strips* off those **nags**
remaining *out with the washing*.

Raider: When, in the past, foreigners arrived on
these shores with horses, it generally spelt trouble
and the thunder of their hooves seems still to stir up
primeval fears and passions. Any runner from foreign parts is to be called a *raider* – the *Czech raider*,
the *Irish raider*, the *French raider. Northern raiders*,
perhaps recalling Jacobites or Vikings, may yet *plun-
der* or *scoop* a big prize on a southern course, though
English horses from places as placid as the West
Country will occasionally fight back: 'The *Devon
raider* looks great each-way **value** for the Scottish
National.' Throughout racing history the martial
idiom has been extended when a *raid* has proved successful: Gladiateur, the French horse that had the
temerity to carry off the Triple Crown in 1865,
became 'the Avenger of Waterloo'.

Rails: The running-rails are worthy of note when all
or part of the field goes the wrong side of them (see
also **doll off**), or in a finish, where it is accepted
wisdom that a horse *under* or *with the rail* to *help* him

is more likely to *run on* than *run about*. *Rails* book-makers are those based in *Members* rather than *Tatts*: the distinction is less important now that they are allowed to display their prices.

Rat-tat-tat: The onomatopoeia designed to replicate the sound of a machine gun (at least in so many of the ropier war poems we remember from school) didn't really do it for us. Perhaps it lends itself better to the *pump-action* of a jockey who hits his horse every stride in a driving finish. Stricter whip laws mean you see or hear it less now, but Lester Piggott's ride on The Minstrel in the 1977 Derby remains a cele-brated example of *rat-tat-tat* whipwork close home, an effort he reprised immediately after coming out of retirement in his win on Royal Academy in the 1990 Breeders' Cup Mile.

Rattle: The *rattle* of hooves rarely seems remarkable in racing, except occasionally when the firmness of the going is emphasised: 'They were really *rattling off* the unwatered ground.' Perhaps horses who *string together* a quick *sequence* of wins are more often described as *rattling* them *up* when prevailing con-ditions are like a *road*: 'Tom George's mare was a prolific winner on the flat in her native Poland, and *rattled up* a four-timer over hurdles this summer.' *Rattle* is also possible as a noun to register a finishing charge in the *dying strides*: 'Distant Thunder came at the winner again with a *real rattle* but the post *came* just too soon.'

Ready to go: This phrase may recall takeaway pizzas or clothes off the peg, but in racing it is used – especially in the winter *game* where patience is required with *store* horses – of animals who can run very quickly after they have been sourced. Here is Keith Reveley, explaining his buying policy after his mother's retirement: 'I needed a few who were *ready to go* to get me established.' *Ready to go on* and *ready made* are parallel phrases, and trainers will often tell a prospective owner that they have in their yard one *ready* to *crack on* or *have some fun* with.

Regulation: The Irish contraction for *regulation fence*, known by the English as an *open ditch*. Peter O'Sullevan usually reminded us of the distinction between *ditches* and what he called *plain fences*, but it seems less insisted upon these days.

Rekindle: So many racehorses, because they have had their share of physical **problems** or because they have simply *fallen out of love* with the **game**, are not as good as they once were. Such horses are encouraged by the verb *rekindle*, which conventionally describes any attempt to revive their fortunes: 'Goblet Of Fire was Listed class on the flat and the switch to hurdles has *rekindled* his *interest*'; 'If Shane Donohue can *rekindle* some of his former **ability** he might be able to win a **little** handicap chase with him.'

Reminder: The classic euphemism for the application of the whip before the race has got **serious**. Although the *smacks* administered can actually be quite hard, *reminders* are always portrayed as an effort to help the horse *concentrate*: 'Joe's just given him a *hurry-up* to keep his *mind on the job*'; 'Carl has *woken him up* with a couple of *reminders.*' Other euphemisms in this vein are *slap down the shoulder* and *tap on the tail*.

Renewal: A pivotal word in a sport with great traditions. Each re-running of an important race brings back into focus the patterns and pointers that have filtered down from the past; and with each recurrence

comes a *renewal* of anticipation. If the upcoming race
looks particularly competitive, it can be described as
a *cracking* or *mouthwatering renewal*. If it looks not
so **hot**, it can be put down as a *sub-standard* or *dis-appointing renewal*. But the expression that best sug-gests the idea of tradition as lifeblood is always going
to be *vintage renewal*. A *vintage edition* of a great race
has something of the same cachet.

Reports: Work-watchers, particularly on Newmarket
Heath, will never be shy of offering *reports* on home
work, which then do the rounds in the racing press:
'Dilshan is *reportedly* pleasing in his work and bang
on course for his pre-season target'; 'Motivator is
reported to be *pulling up trees* at home.' If a horse runs
badly on the racecourse, connections will either vol-unteer or be asked to give information: 'The jockey
reported that the gelding *made a noise*'; 'The trainer
reported that the mare finished *distressed*.' Such
official *reports* give some protection against accusa-tions of **schooling** *in public*. On Irish racecourses,
punters tend to be none the wiser when they hear the
announcement: 'The stewards accepted the trainer's
explanation that there was no explanation.'

Reproduction: 'A *reproduction* of his Newcastle form
should see him *go* very *close* today.' An extremely
common formula in tipping columns, perhaps with
the tacit understanding that the reason bookmakers
make profits is that horses rarely *reproduce* their form
exactly.

Reputation: Tends to take *big*, *tall* or *home* and is
used of a potential **talking horse** of whom **reports**
from the gallops have not yet been entirely vindicated
by performances on the racecourse: 'Racing Demon
has a *tall reputation* at Henrietta Knight's stable and
promises to *improve for* this longer **trip**.'

Ride out: Jockeys *ride out* in the mornings for trainers who *retain* them; when working in the afternoons
they can sometimes get fined for not *riding out* a
horse to the line. In race-reading, *ridden* is a shorthand for 'off the bridle' and *ridden out* a very common way of saying 'just needed to be **pushed out**
to win'.

Ring: 'Backed to take some £50,000 out of the *ring*,
the five-year-old prevailed by half a length.' The
metonym for the body of on-course bookmakers, even
if we can think of no English racecourse where the
main *betting ring* in **Tatts** is circular in shape. No
matter, *ring* is still a suggestive word with its connotations of valiant gladiators going in to do battle against
the odds, or of a masonic circle of practitioners
(Ladbrokes is the *magic sign*).

Rip up your slip: 'If you've backed General Pershing,
you can *rip up your slips*.' A brave commentator may
occasionally be prepared to tempt fate with this kind
of injunction to punters when he spots a well-backed
favourite *toiling in rear*. And sometimes, in the after-
math of a day's racing, the on-course presenter will
remark that the *sea* of *ripped up* betting slips *tells its
own story*. The detritus in **Tatts** can bear eloquent wit-
ness to tattered hopes and such a sight is comparable
to Pope's evocation of ephemeral political pamphlets
'flutt'ring on the rails of Bedlam and Soho'. Except
that Market Rasen on a Tuesday does not provide
quite the same *frisson* as names like those.

Rising: As all thoroughbred racehorses in the northern hemisphere have their birthdays on 1 January,
you often see towards the end of the calendar year
references to horses who are '*rising* four' or '*rising*
eleven'. If a stallion's progeny are having success on
the racecourse, he can be described as a *rising* sire,

provoking the odd titter from those who therefore
picture him preparing for his duties.

Road: Provides a simile for very firm, possibly dangerous ground (*hard* would be the honest official
going description): 'It's riding like a *road* out there
and I'm pulling my fellow out of the big one.' We have
also seen comparisons of bone-dry conditions to an
airport runway, a *go-kart track* and a *pub car park*.
Note though that a minority of horses positively *love
hearing* their hooves **rattle**, even if their handlers
may be prone to a degree of exaggeration: 'He hates
ground with any *give* and needs it like an *absolute
road* to be seen at his best.'

Roll about drunk: Jockeys would never of course be
found *rolling about drunk* and certainly not on a long-
haul flight. But the metaphor may come in handy
towards the end of a marathon race (or any race at
Towcester), as jockeys try to *hold together* horses who
are *out on their feet* and staggering to the finish. The
metaphor can then be re-enacted by racegoers as they
leave the course after the **lucky last**.

Romp: A good verb for indicating a **facile** victory:
'Dance Design fairly *romped home*.' The noun is also
useful to refer to a succession of such victories: 'Celtic
Son completed a *four-timer* on his return to novice
company after three handicap *romps*.' Almost enough
romps to be of interest to the tabloids at this point.

Roots: The most graphic way of saying that a horse
has got in *too deep into* or *too close* to a fence:
'Klondike Charger really *got into the roots* of the fifth
from home.'

Rough off: 'The *pot* at Aintree is tempting but I'm
going to *rough* him *off* now.' An alternative to **put**

away, with more emphasis on the fact that a horse
retired for the season will be *put out* to *grass*, and will
therefore *put on* **condition**. In Australia, a *roughie* is
not a horse kept outside the yard but an outsider in a
race, probably so called because he only has a *rough*
chance of winning: 'Apprentice Ronnie Stewart came
of age as he got everything out of *roughie* Shamrock
Shore to *snare* the feature at Randwick.'

Round here: Specifically used for *course specialists*,
in a very common phrase: 'He absolutely *loves it
round here.*' Means the horse is alleged to adore running around the track rather than that the view of
the surrounding countryside from the horsebox
soothes him on the way there. *Course specialists* can
also be said to *know their way around* a particular
track or, if they are trained nearby, to have *local
knowledge*.

Roust up: 'Paul Eddery had to *roust* him *up* as
early as the mile pole.' This word, used in racing more
than anywhere else, originally meant 'to roar' and,
while jockeys do indeed shout encouragement at
their mounts, it is what they are doing with their
hands and heels that tends to **set** a horse **alight**.
Horses who have received the full **treatment** may
also be interested to learn that it was American
slang for the robust interrogation of suspects by the
police.

Rule Four: Always *applies* when a horse has been
withdrawn before the field comes **under starter's
orders**, leading to a deduction on winning bets linked
to the price of the withdrawn horse. There seems also
to be an unofficial rule that in any big handicap with
seventeen runners, an overnight withdrawal will
always ensure that the layers face each-way liabilities
only on the first three *home*.

Run about: Prepositions, those willing footsoldiers of racing prose, are marshalled in different ways when horses *run*, as the next few entries will show. Horses *run about*, not in all directions, but when they *wander* off a straight line, especially in the closing stages when they become unbalanced or *run away* from the whip: 'Although Alan Munro *pulled* his **stick** *through*, the horse *ran about* under pressure.'

Run away: We have put together three instances of this verb to suggest how the sense can shift as a race proceeds. The first is from a pre-race situation, where the horse in effect 'runs off', except that *run away* is the technically accepted term for this occurrence: 'He tried to *run away* with me going down to the start, but in the race itself ran well.' During the race the verb can indicate how well a horse is going, but the usage will now be a touch ironic in view of the more established meaning: 'He was still *running away* with me coming down to the furlong pole.' Our third example is ironic to the point of being paradoxical, as the jockey reflects on a race lost: 'He didn't make a mistake, but just found the ground *running away* from him.'

Run down: The phrase to describe a horse *getting in* very close to a fence, thus losing momentum (especially if – as is often the case – he then jumps markedly to one side): 'Inglis Drever prevailed **under** McCoy despite *running down* the final two flights.' On the flat the same verb can be used to register a fast-finishing horse *touching off* the leader close home: 'Rebel Rebel *ran down* Capable Guest.'

Run his race: Means to *run* either up to form or out of gas, depending on the context: 'The form is questionable but Private Benjamin has *run his race* in third'; 'Hi Fi made a *short-lived effort* but had *run his* *race* by the second last.' When a horse *comes to run his race*, as the commentator will observe it, we are in the final stages of the **argument**.

Run on: A ubiquitous phrase in race-reading to indicate that a horse has found something *for* **pressure**: 'Always prominent, ridden over 3f out, edged right over 1f out, led well inside final furlong, *ran on well.*' The adverb usually indicates that the horse *found* enough to win, whereas if he just continued at *the* **one pace** you would tend to say *kept on* and if he got a second wind you would say *stayed on*. There is a sharp difference between an animal *running on through* tired horses and one who keeps *pulling out* a bit more.

Run on its merits: Jockeys and trainers will face a ban if they fail to ensure that the runners for which they are responsible do this. There are various symptoms of failure to conform, like **tender** *handling* or using *air shots*. The following is a fairly typical line of defence: 'Murphy said his **instructions** had been to take his time as the gelding had run very **green** last time.' Now that enquiries are open to the press, the Jockey Club is keen to avoid any suggestion of tender handling on its own account, as journalists attending disciplinary hearings have been quick to observe: 'Those who take on the Club in a state of legal undress get whipped hardest.' *Air shots* are out of order, as we said.

S

Sand: Still a synonym for *all-weather*, even if fibre-sand surfaces are being replaced by Polytrack. Those who call it racing *on the sand* ensure that it does not sound entirely serious, even if such racing never quite sinks to the level of a *donkey-derby*: 'Before the *turf* action starts next week, the *sand lovers* have their day in the sun with the big *card* at Lingfield today.'

Sandwich: In a big field, horses can be running so close together that they jump three or four abreast, often with unfortunate results: 'Bewleys Berry was an extremely unlucky *faller* as he found himself in the middle of a mid-air *sandwich* with no chance of staying on his feet.' In live commentary, Bewleys Berry might have been described as the *meat* in the *sandwich*, and if unfortunate enough to be running in Belgium he might have become it.

Satchel: 'The layers will be *filling their satchels* after that shock result.' A canonical expression: even professionals are still liable to bet in cash and large amounts of *readies* go in and out of the bags on a bookmaker's *joint*. That we think the battered old bags looked more like holdalls than *satchels*, and that most present-day *joints* have a plastic wheelie-bin as the receptacle for cash, is probably, to use an equally makeshift expression, par for the course.

Saver: 'I've had a little *saver* on Reckless Fred.' What punters say when they have a supplementary bet, usually *each way*, to *cover* themselves if their main selection *flops*. There are certain types of punter, conservative or self-deluded or both, who seem to have had a *covering bet* on every horse in the race.

Scene: At the end of a contest, if **waited with**, a horse may suddenly enter the script: 'Monte Cristo *arrived on the scene* full of running, clearly **travelling** better'; 'After *coming late* on the *scene* to beat Clear Dawn by a length, the popular ten-year-old was

treated to a rousing reception.' If in these circumstances a horse should finish placed, it can be said to
have been *on the premises*.

Scenic route: Rather hyperbolic way of saying that
a jockey is steering a course on the outside of the field
or, perhaps in search of better ground, has *ploughed a
lone furrow* detached from the remainder: 'Olly
McPhail is taking the *scenic route* on Tiraldo.'
Whereas if the jockey goes *round the houses*, he will,
in the absence of *splits*, have been forced to come
with his run on the wide outside.

School: The proper term for teaching a horse to jump,
and for keeping his *eye in* once he has been taught:
'We *schooled* him over three fences in the week and he
was foot-perfect'. *Loose schooling*, for all the evocations
of St Trinian's, means that the horse's home work
involves jumping on a *lunge-rein*. *Schooling in public*,
an offence under both codes, describes the situation
when connections put the importance of giving
their horses an *educational* run ahead of achieving the
best possible placing. Sometimes the possibility of a
lenient handicap mark may more or less imperceptibly
influence a trainer in his desire to teach patiently.

Scoot: Used when a horse *asked a question* provides
an immediate response and quickly puts distance
between himself and the rest: 'Back In Front *scooted
up* at Naas'; 'Definate Spectacle *scooted away* for an
eight-length success.' The most typical formulation,
though, is *scoot clear*, which forms a series with *bound
clear* and *skip clear*.

Scope: A racing key word. The prevailing sense is of
a good physical specimen with the potential to *go on*
improving: 'Kevin Ryan has a nice mixed bunch of
two-year-olds, some of them *sharp* but others more

scopey and in need of time.' However, sometimes there can be a disconnection between size and the potential to remain *unexposed*: 'My fellow hasn't got the *scope* of some of these but there's some *improvement* in him.' See also **dirty**.

Scrape: Jockeys *scraping the paint* are hugging the inside rail, rather than taking the **scenic route**, in order to save ground. They can also be described as taking the *shortest way round*. Horses, especially if they are well-backed favourites, can be said to *scrape* or *clamber home* if they prevail unimpressively.

Scratch: The obvious word to describe withdrawing a horse from an engagement, but employed also to evoke the action of an animal who is not the best of *movers*: 'Illustrious Duke really *scratched* his way down to the start so let's hope he'll move more freely at racing pace.'

Screens: These are *green* in Britain and *dreaded* anywhere they are used, since they are erected around a stricken horse. Racecards tend to inform the racing public that the *screens* are there to protect the *privacy* of the horse and connections, although we cannot help thinking that they are there more to protect the sensibilities of the British horse-lover. If things turn out not as bad as first feared, a friendly little joke is sometimes allowed: 'The **old** soldier was only winded and when he saw the *screens* going up he soon got to his **feet**.'

Scrub along: 'Mattie Bachelor's *low* in the saddle *scrubbing him along* already.' The action here is similar to **punching** *out* a horse, with the difference that the commentator probably does not think the horse is going to win. Hence, perhaps, the menial flavour of the image.

Search party: Jim McGrath was the first commentator we heard use this expression, which is a wonderful way of informing the crowd that the stragglers
at the back of a field (usually over a long distance in
the *mud*) are unlikely to *complete* and certainly will
not threaten the leaders: 'Pop Abroad is weakening
and you'll have to send out a *search party* for the
remainder.'

Seconditis: 'Thisthatandtother has had an appalling
bout of *seconditis.*' The reportable, though not strictly
notifiable, disease afflicting any horse who has run
up a sequence of 2s before his name – five in a row in
the case quoted. A horse with this problem can also
be said to keep *finding one too good* for him. Compare
shop horse for an expression produced by a string of
1s in the form.

Send out: Trainers are said to *send out* winners far
more frequently than they *bring* them *home*, unless a
National winner *comes home* to a hero's welcome.

Serious: The adjective features in one of the many
euphemistic phrases for the moment in a race when
the jockey starts to give his mount *vigorous encouragement*: 'George Duffield begins to *get serious* on
Environment Friend over on the far rail.' A slightly
longer version, which is therefore used less in live
commentary, is *to ask serious questions*. Therefore a
facile victory can be signalled in the following
way: 'Silence Reigns landed the hunters' chase with
Colman Sweeney never having to *get serious.*' At the
same time, because racing really is a *serious* business
(even for many animals bought as *fun horses*), the
word sheds its euphemistic purpose to become almost
a paradigm for the sport in its day-to-day operations:
'He's a very *serious* horse'; 'That last run was *serious*
form'; 'He did a *serious* piece of work this morning';

'We'll have to train him *seriously* for the Grand National now.'

Servant: 'October Mist has been a *grand servant* to this yard and **owes** *us nothing*.' For once, this expression has the connections–horse relationship about right. *Servant* seems to take **grand** more than *fine* in racing parlance.

Set alight: Useful for registering the moment in a race when the rider exerts pressure and his mount responds: 'Frankie Norton *sets him alight* and he's **scooted** *clear*.' More generally, the phrase can be used of anything that **rekindles** a horse's enthusiasm: 'His trainer put this much better run down to an outing with the Bicester Hunt, which apparently *set him alight*.'

Setback: For some reason preferred to 'injury', maybe because of the idea of being *held up* in your **work**, maybe because subconsciously racing journalism thinks in terms of the aspirations of the connections as much as the welfare of the horses: 'Chaille Chaille announced that Ambobo had suffered a *setback* and would miss the Festival.' If a trainer rings an owner to inform him his horse has had a *little setback*, there is always the possibility that the animal will never be *seen out* again.

Set it up: Frontrunners, no doubt unwittingly or unintentionally, can do this to a race for **hold-up horses** able to exploit with a *turn of foot*: 'Indien Royal forced a fast pace which ultimately *set it up* for the more experienced Almaydan.'

Settle: A jockey's role in *settling* his mount early in a race can be just as important as his *urgings* in the closing stages. Hence the number of metaphors available for a **keen** horse and the fact that if he is successfully restrained he will tend to be described as *beautifully* or *nicely settled*.

Shake the reins: 'I dropped my *stick* and I could only *shake the reins* at him then.' Jockeys often seem to say this when they lose their whips, apparently acknowledging how **hands and heels** are much less effective than a dose of the **beater**. The phrase can also be used to indicate how little **assistance** a *classy* horse needs from his pilot: 'All it needed was a *shake of the reins* and Nashwan was quickly clear.'

Shake up: This is one of those tricky little phrasal verbs that needs interpreting according to the context. Sometimes it will mean the jockey applying reasonably restrained **punching**: 'Menhoubah only had to be *shaken up* to score.' On other occasions it can imply *strong driving* with use of the whip: 'Supple really had to *shake* Mutafanen *up* to get his mind on the job.' The noun *shake-up* serves, like in other sports, as a way of referring to the *closing stages* and is not an announcement that one of the Maktoums will be taking the ride.

Shape: The most common verb of all for referring to a promising performance, especially on a seasonal debut or over a new **trip**: 'Piccolomini *shaped* with promise when third over seven furlongs on his Musselburgh debut.' Meanwhile the noun can work to record appreciation of proficient jumping – 'We've tried him over poles and tyres and he makes a *good, old shape*' – or of a *well-framed* handicap: 'There's a *nice shape* to the showcase race, with many of the runners *holding* good chances *at the weights*.'

Sharp: Adjective used to describe racetracks with *tight* and/or frequent bends which suit the *handy*,

nippy type (as opposed to *galloping **sorts*** who prefer
stiff or, as logic would have it, *galloping* tracks): 'He
needs a *sharp* two miles and Taunton is right up his
street.' Horses can be *sharpened up* by a previous run
or by the *application* of blinkers.

Sheepskin noseband: A *sheepskin noseband* (or
shadow check in the States) is designed to keep a hard-
pulling horse's head down. Such a *noseband* may not
strictly be considered a piece of **headgear** (it does
not have to be declared like *sheepskin cheekpieces*) but
it is a signature of certain trainers such as Andrew
Balding and Noel Chance, and it is usually pointed
out fondly by commentators eager to help their viewers pick the runners out: 'River City's the one in the
sheepskin noseband.' Note that the fact the *noseband* is
made of *sheepskin* is almost always remarked upon,
even though there seem to be no alternative materials
available.

Shirk the issue: 'Mustang Ali was never allowed to
shirk the issue by Tony Culhane.' *Shirking the issue* is
another way of saying a horse will not *go through*
with its *effort* at the **business end** of a race. Similar
ideas are *raising the white flag* and *crying enough*.

Shop horse: A phrase used, with some condescen-
sion, by professional pundits to describe a horse
who has a string of 1s to his form. The inference is
that this may attract **mug** punters making a cursory
inspection of the racecard in the *offices*, but that the
wins in question do not stand up to inspection when
contextualised by the *grade* at which the *shop horse*
has been aimed on this occasion.

Short: We have noted this word in three particular
situations. Firstly, describing an animal as a *short
horse* has nothing to do with how many *hands* he

stands. The issue is rather whether such an animal will get home over the *trip* in prospect: 'Champion Chasers need to stay and *short* runners regularly get found out.' Then, there are times when a trainer preparing a horse for a main target will deliberately leave himself something to work on: 'It is likely Hobbs left Rooster Booster a little *short* at Sandown.' Finally, of course, certain jockeys ride *short*.

Short one: The *one* in this expression is a *stride*, which is what horses *put in* when they *fiddle* a fence or, less auspiciously, when they *put down* on their jockeys if *asked* for a big one. Jim McGrath shortens to *shorty*.

Shrewd: Used of trainers or connections, sometimes with more than a whiff of meaning 'b–nt'.

Shuffle: Horses are much more often *shuffled back* by the *pack* rather than *up* by their jockeys, who will probably find it difficult to *play* their mounts in these circumstances. But there are exceptions: 'Mahtoum was *shuffled back* to last early and couldn't get a clear run, but Darren Beadman kept his cool and the gelding produced a *withering* late burst.' The cards go back to the dealer when a *prep race* changes the complexion of an ante-post market: 'The *trial* caused more *shuffling* in the Champion Hurdle market, with Macs Joy *trimmed* to 8s and Hardy Eustace *nudged out* to 10/1.'

Shutters: 'Tony McCoy is coming in for *plenty* of rides despite the *shutters being up* at Jonjo O'Neill's yard.' When there is *coughing* in the stable, and the trainer decides not to *send out* runners until his *inmates* are *well in themselves* again, this is the usual metaphor. In real life, though, the *shutters* and *top doors* will tend to be left open in such circumstances to allow as much fresh air as possible into the yard.

We have seen another image, certainly a visual cliché in movies, to paint a picture of how the same training operation has been laid low: 'The *tumbleweed* has been blowing through O'Neill's yard for virtually the last six months.'

Side door: Often the exit route for jockeys when they are *unseated*, after they have tried to *cling on* desperately: 'Barry Fenton's *come out* the *side door* there after nearly pulling off a miraculous recovery.'

Sir: 'No, *sir*!', 'Please, *sir*!', 'Let me turn, *sir*!': jump jockeys lining up at the start of a big race with many runners can still sound like inhabitants of an almshouse begging for gruel. They can also still expect to be addressed by their surnames, perhaps a legacy of the fact that starters have tended to be military men. This is a contrast to the courtesies extended at Daytona: 'Gentlemen, start your engines.' Even though the starts of jump races are now more frequently entrusted to veterans of the *weighing room* rather than the officers' mess, somehow standards appear to have been maintained.

Sit: The shorthand for a jockey keeping his mount *settled* until the right moment, usually the last possible moment. The phrase can be used very neutrally in commentary: 'Neil Callan still choosing to *sit* on Sovereignty.' But because races are so often lost by getting to the front *too soon*, the idea will often be amplified in post-mortems, whether you win or lose: 'I really had to *sit and suffer* but I knew I had to *come on the scene* very late as he *idles* in front'; 'It was my fault he got beaten last time out because I should have told Conor O'Dwyer to *sit and sit*.' Sometimes jump jockeys have no other option: 'Richard Johnson was forced to *sit tight* when his mount made two major blunders.' When they *accept the situation*, riders can

be said to *sit up*, in that they are no longer adopting
the *drive position* but coming home in their own time.

Sketchy: Rather a neat word for a horse that still has
some learning to do over obstacles: 'Be Upstanding's
sketchy jumping undermines confidence'; 'Zimbabwe
reverts to hurdles after jumping *sketchily*.' *Iffy* is
hardly less neat as a substitute.

Skinner: 'Dabiroun was a complete *skinner* for the
bookies in the last.' Possibly Australian in origin, this
colloquialism is used for a long-odds winner who
fills the layers' *satchels* while conceivably taking the
shirts off punters' backs.

Slash: What bookmakers do to *odds* if they reduce
them drastically: 'The sponsors were clearly impressed,
slashing him to 12/1 for the big one.' There are more
expressive alternatives, as in: 'Totesport *took the shears*
to Ulaan Baatar's Arkle Chase odds.' If the price had
been reduced less dramatically, it would have been *cut*
or *trimmed*.

Sloppy: In Britain and Ireland reserved for *sloppy*
rounds of jumping; in North America and Australasia
used to describe track conditions in which the horses
are going through a *sloppy* top surface where there
is standing water: 'Quest also won this year's Lure
Handicap *in the slop* at Gulfstream.'

Sluice: You don't hear this verb very much in con-
temporary English, but it can makes an appearance if
a racehorse wins impressively, particularly when the
ground is *bottomless*: 'Regal Ambition *sluiced through*
the Chepstow *mud* to become ante-post favourite for
the Sun Alliance'; 'In Divine Gift Jarvis saddles a colt
lightly raced since *sluicing up* in the conditions race
on Lincoln day in 2004.'

Small but select field: Sometimes racecourse executives, sponsors or commentators can lament the *disappointing turnout*, particularly if it is for a *decent prize*. But more often than not, especially if they are trying to stop the viewer turning over to the twenty-runner handicap on the other channel, they will emphasise the quality over the quantity: 'Only three *stood their ground* overnight; nevertheless it's a *small but select field.*'

Smash into: Jumpers can *smash into* fences, but the much more common usage is to describe any ambitious-looking move by a punter: 'My best contact in Ireland has advised me to *smash into* this very well-handicapped **beast** at Kempton.' This example is typical in that the gambler is said to *smash into* the horse not the bookmakers.

Smuggle: 'Murphy *smuggled* Celestial Gold round at the rear as if out for a Sunday **hack**.' This verb acknowledges the talent of a jockey who manages to *switch off* a horse who needs restraint and **travels** round almost unnoticed until the **business end** of the race. If the horse was considered to be **well in**, this just adds to the clandestine flavour of the ride.

Snatches: 'Fiddling The Facts is *running in snatches.*' First-time racegoers tend to find this expression funny because of the *double entendre* (the alternative *gone in snatches* tickles them even more). In fact, it is a perfectly serious way of describing a horse who comes *on* and *off* the *bridle*. Everybody has a favourite horse who had a *tendency* to *run in snatches*. Our candidate is Bonanza Boy, multiple winner of the Welsh National, and also winner of the Racing Post Chase when coming from *another **parish***. When a jockey *snatches up*, it means he has had to *apply the brakes* very quickly by pulling on the bit. Almost invariably he is *forced* to do so by another rider *taking his ground*.

Social climber: This little metaphor can become fashionable if a horse of lowly origins has success on the racecourse (or more rarely at stud) against more *blue-blooded **sorts***: 'Attraction is supposedly humbly bred, but has been the *social climber* of the year.'

Sort: A curious way of referring to horses as well as to human beings, but whereas in the latter cases the noun might be qualified negatively – 'He's an odd *sort*' – it is more likely to be affirmative in racing: 'He's an ***admirable** sort*'; 'She's a lovely ***forward** sort.*' The same observation might be made of the word *type*: compare neighbours twitching at the net curtains and saying 'I don't like their *type*' with trainers patting their horses' necks and praising them as 'most likeable *types*'.

Sort themselves out: A handy filler in commentary which more often than not means the commentator is trying to sort himself out rather than the horses: 'And as they *sort themselves out* through the first furlong . . .' ('I'm ***paddling***' might be the subtext here.)

Sound: There are many qualities required of the racehorse but one of the most important is *soundness*, which comes ahead even of being ***tough***. Quite simply, if a horse is *sound*, it is not lame. Note therefore an extra resonance in racing when a trainer hopes his inmate comes home *safe and sound*. *Soundness* does not normally need qualification or amplification, although nervous trainers may occasionally supply a simile: 'After their ***serious*** piece of work, it was a big relief when I looked them over this morning and found them as *sound as bells*.'

Sparkle: 'He's been a bit *on and off* this season and didn't really *sparkle* last time'; 'Fallon said afterwards that Motivator lacked a bit of the *sparkle* he'd been showing at home.' Curiously, trainers only seem to use the word *sparkle* when they are remarking upon the lack of it, so that *sparkling* form is not a particularly common expression in racing.

Special: Works almost as a synonym for **serious** when a trainer is talking up one of his *charges*: 'I've trained a few nice two-year-olds but this one could be a little bit *special*.' Also used of jockeys when they pull off a win with the style of riding they have become famous for: 'The horse benefited from a Timmy Murphy *special* in being **waited with** off a strong pace before **picking off** tiring rivals late on.'

Spell: In Britain and Ireland the word *break* tends to cover either a short period intra-season when a horse is given some time away from the track or the longer period when he is **roughed off** for the season. In Australia the distinction is made clearer: form guides will refer to a horse being *freshened* in the first case and being given a *spell* or *spelled* in the second: 'The win earned Shamrock Shore a trip to the *spelling paddock* and Thomsen said he will now turn his sights to a winter carnival campaign and possible berth in the Brisbane Cup.'

Splendid isolation: 'A *soft race*, which resulted in Diplomatic Gamble coming home in *splendid isolation* after making **virtually** all.' A term coined in relation to British foreign policy used to compliment a *wide-margin* winner. Occasionally, we may spot a reporter naming the next horse in the *chasing* **pack** in an almost mechanical way: 'Alan O'Keeffe **booted** News Maker *on* around the turn and the partnership won in *splendid isolation* from Metal Detector.' On the other hand, we can sense a certain striving for rhetorical effect in this celebration of Hedgehunter's triumph in the National, the horse having fallen at the last the year before: 'This time he *soared* over the fence as though he had *just jumped in* and set off up the run-in like a ***spring-heeled*** two-year-old in *splendid isolation*.' For runners who race in *isolation* at the other end of the field, different terms are called for, and many are available – see ***washing***, ***search party***.

Splits: Over jumps, commentators can occasionally say that a horse who spreadeagles *on landing* has *done the splits*. More common though is the usage on the flat to denote ***traffic*** *trouble* or the absence of it: 'She ran really well at Salisbury last time out but just didn't get the *splits*'; 'Darryl found the *split* a furlong from home and the horse did the rest.' Meanwhile, trainers with two runners in the same race may need to be careful not to upset the different sets of connections (or may be trying to lengthen the odds of the more fancied animal): 'They're both very nice horses and I can't *split* them at home.'

Split-screen: No race you see beamed into a betting shop is too important to be interrupted by that familiar announcement: 'The hare's on the move at Catford: *split-screen*!' There is indeed no room for sentimentality in the *offices*, where the turnover of betting opportunities is remorseless. One summer day many years ago in a Cambridge branch of Corals we heard the following over the *blower*: 'And confirmation from Auteuil that the fall to Dawn Run was fatal. At Monmore they bet . . .'

Spring-heeled: '*Spring-heeled* Spinofski led his rivals a *merry dance*.' A way of saying a horse jumped in spectacular fashion (though it can also be suggested by bursts of acceleration on the flat). The idea can easily be cranked up further: 'The way he jumped today it was as if he had *rocket boosters* on his back legs.' ***Pogo-sticks*** are in a different category.

Squiggle horse: Such is the influence of Timeform, the most prominent of British racing's rating agencies, that its symbol for an 'unreliable' horse has become a recognised shorthand for a horse with temperamental difficulties. A double *squiggle* used to be defined as an 'arrant rogue or thorough jade, so temperamentally unsatisfactory as to be not worth a rating'. If their horse is awarded the *dreaded Timeform squiggle* connections can naturally take umbrage, although some are philosophical: 'There's no way he's a *squiggle horse* the way he ran today. He slogged his guts out'; 'OK, he's a *squiggle horse* but he's won his fair share of races.' In America, *Beyer* speed ratings are as influential as Timeform ratings over here, and as likely to upset those with a vested interest: 'I don't think Greater Good has gotten the respect because he hasn't run a fast *Beyer*. I'm thinking that if they run a 105 *Beyer* against him, he'll run a 106.'

Stag: Features in the requisite simile for really good jumping: 'Kissane jumped like an absolute *stag* in the Reynoldstown.' This may add extra resonance to the clichés available for horses ***matching strides*** in a race – 'Monty's Double made a ***bold bid*** to *lock horns* with the winner' – or of two horses taking each other on when connections *stand their ground*: 'Fundamentalist *locks horns* again with My Will in the Dipper' (in this particular example Fundamentalist sadly did not jump like a *stag*). The French apparently prefer to compare such horses to *cats*, perhaps because stone walls are still *there to be jumped* on French tracks.

Stalking: The *stalking horse* is nearly always metaphorical these days, and suited more to Downing

Street than to Down Royal. But, very occasionally, associated tactics can be employed on the track: the riding of Golden Freeze in the 1992 Gold Cup to disturb the jumping *rhythm* of Carvill's Hill is a notorious example. However, it is quite acceptable for jockeys to *stalk* their prey in the sense of riding a *waiting* race: 'That was another typical Timmy Murphy *stalking* ride.'

Stand up: 'If he *stands up*, he'll win today.' The kind of oversimplification born of a trainer's confidence, or nerves, although the statement does seem properly applicable to Moscow Flyer, whose form figures as a chaser until his defeat at Punchestown read F111F11-1U111U-111U11-111111 (compare *more letters than numbers*). During a race, if a horse has been *left* clear, you would tend to use a slightly different formulation: 'Two left to jump and it looks as if he only has to *stay on his feet* to take the prize.' Meanwhile, stallions simply *stand* at stud, in more ways than one.

Steamer: The standard expression (indeed the noun sometimes takes the adverb *proverbial*) when a horse for whom initial **whispers** have created a wall of money is backed *off the boards*: 'There's a *steamer* developing in this race in the form of Arcalis.' An alternative is *springer*.

Steering job: A ride where the horse goes so well that the jockey does not need to **roust** him to induce forward momentum and just has to *put* him in the right place to come through. Tipping lines in particular promise *absolute steering jobs* each morning; by the afternoon the jockey in question is often seen administering the full **treatment** seconds into the race when the horse doesn't go a *yard*. The verb can be used, more commonly overseas, as a neutral synonym for *ride*: 'Felix Coetzee, who *steers* the *speedster* through his races, is unflustered about the draw.'

Step up: What horses do when they tackle a longer *trip* or a higher *grade*. If going in the reverse direction, they never seem to 'step down' but *drop back* in distance or *drop down* in class.

Stick: The most common synonym for *whip*, particularly when a jockey *picks* it *up*, *pulls* it *through* to his other hand or, unfortunately, drops it. *Bat* and *wand* are alternatives, while the colourful options are *beater* and *persuader*. In the plural, the noun is a colloquialism for obstacles: 'And in the evening meetings, they *go* at Wolverhampton and over the *sticks* at Taunton.' The adjective *sticky* is used of *gluey* ground, or of bad jumping (it may be no coincidence that one often causes the other).

Stoke up: Whereas most metaphors associated with the rider *getting serious* compare horses to the motorised vehicles that replaced them in a historical sense, the occasional one harks back to the halcyon days of steam: 'Richard Quinn was *stoking* the favourite *up* over four furlongs out, but the favourite stuck to his task and *landed the spoils.*'

Stop: The most well-known meaning is to *stop* a horse *running on its merits*: 'It was alleged, though never proven, that Playschool had been *stopped* in the Gold Cup.' But when trainers in both codes are convincing themselves that one of their horses will get a longer *trip*, they say things like: 'He wasn't *stopping* at the end of a mile last time out, so I think he'll *get* ten furlongs.' Similarly *not stopping* is synonymous with not *coming back* to your field: 'One Man was *not stopping*, and to whoops of joy from the crowd set off up the hill to beat Or Royal.' However, there are

occasions when doubtful stayers or *bleeders stop* as if
they have been *shot*.

Straight: In racing means *fit*, rather than 'not b–nt':
'Through The Rye will definitely *come on* for the run,
but he's as *straight* as I can get him at home.'

Straightforward: When an animal is not *straightforward* it means he is a **difficult ride**: 'Ever So
Charming is not a *straightforward ride* and looks the
type who needs **headgear**.' But a horse who is
straightforward has a few more qualities than being
biddable: he is usually a pleasure to have anything to
do with at home; he keeps his head in the **manger**; he
does everything that is asked of him; he has a most
likeable **attitude**. Most importantly, he tends not to *go
wrong*.

Streetwise: Despite the fact that *classy* animals
would never be risked on ground as hard as a **road**,
their trainers are very happy to hear them described
as *streetfighters* or *streetwise* to indicate that they can
look after themselves, especially in the *hurly-burly* of
big handicaps: 'Royal Shakespeare has it *all to do* off
top weight but we have to get him *streetwise* if we're
going to Cheltenham.'

Stride: What horses need to *see* before a fence, and
what jockeys sometimes think they see, often with
disastrous results: 'Remittance Man really *saw a stride*
there and jumped it from *outside the **wings**'*; 'Barry
saw a stride but the horse just didn't **pick up** for him.'
On the flat, the *lengthening* or *shortening stride* of a
horse is a tell-tale sign of (or sometimes just a tired
metaphor for) exhaustion. A *stride* can also be a unit
of measure for the pace of a race – as in 'They possibly went a *stride* too quick for him' – or the index of
an impressive performance. It is extraordinary, in

fact, how many races are apparently settled in just a *matter of strides*. More elegant, though, as a way of marking the climactic finish to a race, is the phrase *in the dying strides*, which can mark also an intrusion of sentiment into the reporting: 'Inglis Drever had to do all the ***donkey work*** and it was cruel that he was ***collared*** *in the dying strides*.'

Strip fitter: A well-worn way of saying that a horse is going to *come on* for the run: 'Definite Approach will *strip fitter* for his previous outing.' An idea probably descended from boxing and apt in the sense that seasoned *paddock watchers* will not get a proper sense of a horse's **condition** until the *rug* is taken off him. Indeed, there is a definite whiff of skulduggery about what is going on in this other example: 'Not only did the 5/2 ***bumper*** favourite enter the parade ring only when his rivals were exiting, but he was also comprehensively *rugged up*.'

Strong: Jockeys who are *strong in the finish* are much sought after by connections, particularly after they think a *stylist* has just lost them a race. (If a trainer tells you, 'Your horse needs a *stronger* jockey,' translate as: 'We're running out of other excuses so let's try blaming today's rider.') Steve Smith Eccles apparently now regrets his observation that lady jockeys are 'about as *strong as half a disprin*' – at least when Clare Balding is in earshot.

Strong Gale: One of the shorthands that can be confusing to the uninitiated is a reference to a horse in training directly by the name of his sire: 'He's a typical *Bustino* in everything he does'; 'He's the first *Strong Gale* I've had and I doubt he'll stay three miles.' Also seen in the plural when trainers – correctly in many cases – confer character traits on each male line: 'With some of these *Roseliers*, you have to be

patient waiting for the ***penny*** *to drop?* It may be
another sign of male chauvinism, or simply reflect the
fact that a single mare can *throw* only so many foals,
that the dam's name is seldom referred to in the same
way: 'Eshan's home work is lazy, just like his mother's.'

Stylish: There need not necessarily be a dichotomy
between ***strong*** and *stylish* jockeys. However, to
describe a rider as a *great stylist*, while praising him for
sitting quietly and being *at one* with his horse, may
sometimes imply that he might not be seen to best effect
on more recalcitrant animals. This tension between
style and strength, and the fact that connections and punters default to a preference for the latter, is brought out by this description of the South
Australian jockey Jim Johnson: 'He could not be
described as *stylish*; when applying *vigor* he appeared *ill-
balanced* and downright ungainly. As a result Jim was
dubbed "the last of the *straightbacks*" or "*Jerky* Jim".
Johnson often *sat upright* in the saddle flourishing his
whip extravagantly, however there was no denying his
effectiveness and his *strength* won many a race when all
seemed lost.'

Super: One of those adjectives that seems to aspire
to adverbial status in racing circles: 'He jumped *super*
and, as my father Pat used to say, you win lots of races
by good jumping out in the ***country?*** ***Grand*** and *great*
behave in a similar way: 'He ***settled*** *great* and jumped
great and I always had a nice *lot of horse* ***under*** me.'
To quote another example with an established prove-
nance: the eighteenth-century trainer William Cowle
handwrote owner Sir James Lowther a letter to convey
the important news that 'Gimcrack won very *easy*'.

Supplement: While it is possible for horses who
have not been entered at the early forfeit stages to
be *supplemented* to certain Group 1 races (on pay-

ment of an appropriately extortionate fee), the most common usage is when a horse is making a *quick reappearance* and a journalist is working in a reference to the previous outing: 'Hopscotch looks to *supplement* her Worcester *gains* over a similar *trip* at Newton Abbot.' When connections are planning a quick second helping in Australia, a different phrase is used: 'Cavanough, who recently moved to Albury from Tocumwal, declared Sheedy's Sheila an acceptor but will wait before deciding if she *backs up* on the opening day of the Albury Cup carnival.'

T

Tactical race: Often means that the runners just went very slowly in the early part of the race, not necessarily that any *tactics* were involved.

Take it in turns to win: Weary punters regularly complain about certain types of race, like sprint handicaps or staying chases, where the implication is that proper study of the form is a waste of time: 'They just *take it in turns to win* these Musselburgh *dashes*.' There is a similar formulation available for a horse who is no longer **ahead of the handicapper**: 'Legal Set is a tough performer but only *wins in his turn* these days.' Even at the highest grade there can be a slight feeling of tedium if no young stars break on to the scene: 'The sprinting division was made up of the "*usual suspects*", according to chief handicapper Nigel Gray, led by Somnus and Var on 117.'

Taken off his feet: An expression for finding it all **happening too quickly** which has everything to do with the fast pace of a race rather than the fact that a horse may be jumping fences: 'Dropping back to the minimum five, he was simply *taken* right *off his feet.*' And here is an example of almost symbiotic identification with the horse from Ginger McCain, recollecting his emotions after Red Rum won his first National: 'It was all very strange to us and it's true to say we were *taken off our legs* a bit.'

Take out: When, as a punter, you are looking to *put* some horses *up against* the *field*, you will often look at one or more previous races with key *collateral* form and *take out* one or two horses from there: 'Kingscliff stayed on resolutely after *blowing up* a mile from home on his first run in 11 months and was the horse most judges *took out* of the race.'

Talking horse: Like so many of those expressions which now have currency outside racing, this one is not actually used that often in the trade. Typically, it describes a horse with a huge *home reputation* which may not be justified. But seen out more than a *stalking* horse.

Tank: A more precise description of certain *machines*: 'He was always going to be a three-year-old and he's filled out into an absolute *tank.*' Also used in those extensive metaphors involving fuel *tanks*. These can be used in a particular race (see *empty*) or when giving details of a horse's *preparation*: 'War Of Attrition is not 100% fit – I've left a good deal in the *tank* with Cheltenham in mind.'

Tatts: If you overhear a well-dressed person on a mobile phone asking, 'Are you going to *Tattersalls*?' they are likely to be bloodstock *agents* persuading their patrons to attend the sales. However, if someone in jeans asks you to meet him in *Tatts* rather than *Members*, he is referring to the enclosure of a racecourse where the main betting ring is situated. The nomenclature of this enclosure derives from the fact that the Subscription Room at Richard Tattersalls' sales office was where one of the earliest organised betting markets on racing formed (*Tattersalls' Rules* on betting, including **Rule Four**, exist to this day). It has often been observed that the three enclosures on a typical British racecourse mirror the British class system: *Members* or *Club* corresponding to upper, *Tatts* to middle and the *Course Enclosure* or *Silver Ring* (so called because it is assumed the bets would be in small change) to working. However, just as class distinctions are much less rigid than they were, so the differences between the enclosures have become less pronounced, especially now that betting on the **rails** is essentially the same experience as betting in *Tatts*. Don't try getting into *Members* at Newbury or Ascot without a tie, though.

Tender: Always goes with *handling*, or else *ride*, as in: 'Quinlan Terry made *eyecatching* late progress under a most *tender ride.*' The best alternatives are *considerate* and *sympathetic*. There is often a suggestion, either veiled or explicit, that *tender handling* amounts to not **trying**. Compare **run on its merits**.

Terms: Before a handicap, tipsters will remind readers that one horse meets another on *better terms* than in a previous race or than if the current contest was going to be a *conditions* event. During the race itself, *on terms* is a synonym for *in contention* but, sadly for connections, the phrase will most regularly turn up in the race-reader's undeceived potted summary: '*never on terms*'. Whereas in the paddock, *on terms* is likely to mean that the horse in question is on *good terms* with **himself**.

Test: 'With all the *speed horses* in the race we decided to make it a *real test.*' *Test of stamina* is automatically

understood to be the meaning here. But other things
can also be *put to the test*, like *Group 1 credentials*,
and the word can be used as a synonym for 'race',
especially when composing a headline of the type:
'Harchibald evens for Kempton *test*'.

The four horse: 'I'm backing the *four horse*'; 'The *six
horse* looks very **well in** at the weights.' A mannered
way of referring to an animal's racecard number borrowed from greyhound racing. Punters will sometimes
recognise the derivation by actually calling a horse *the
two dog*. Another word to have crossed tracks is *trap*
when referring to a horse's draw: 'There is some pace
on the far side with the likes of Always Esteemed
in *trap* nine.' If connections of a **hold-up horse** employ
a pacemaker, the *hare* may even be seen *running*
at Ascot.

Thinker: The Thinker, winner of the 1987 Gold Cup,
was not actually a *thinker*, since this term refers to a
horse who, to the exasperation of his connections, will
not go through the pain barrier: 'He's a bit of a *thinker*
and the *application* of the *blinds* has had little effect.'
The homophony with the word *tinker* can make this
term seem more pejorative – particularly in places like
Thurles: 'He's a real *thinker* and we're scratching our
heads about what to do with him.' The verb can also
turn up, as in this intriguing example: 'He tends to
think a bit at the end of his races.'

Thread: A standard metaphor in race previews:
'Abalvino can pick up the *winning thread* again now
he is *dropped* into handicap **company**.' Jockeys on
hold-up horses can also be commended for the way
they *thread* or *weave* their mount *through* the field.

Thrown in: Often with *at the weights* added to
suggest that a horse is very much a handicap *good*

thing: 'Captain Scott looks absolutely *thrown in* off 8 stone 2.' If you are *chucked in* you are obviously a *very good thing*. But on other occasions, especially when novices are *thrown straight in* to handicap ***company***, the assignment is much stiffer. In breeding, mares *throw* their offspring, whereas sires *get* their progeny.

Tic-tac: The language of hand signals used by book-makers for over a hundred years to telegraph prices to different parts of the course so that they are not caught by sudden market movements elsewhere. Modern technology is threatening the future of *tic-tac* as an art-form but John McCririck has done much to keep its language alive in his sparkling reports from the ring. When demonstrating that a horse is on the ***drift***, he will be seen going *up the arm* (11/8) to *earhole* (6/4) to *top of the head* (2/1). During Big Mac's appearances on *Celebrity Big Brother* we also saw him going finger to nostril, but we don't know what this means in *tic-tac*.

Tilt: Despite the chivalric connotations, the noun can be used quite neutrally in pre-race journalism to mean that connections will enter a particular race: 'Non So may *bypass* the Bonusprint in favour of a *tilt* at the Jenny Mould Memorial Chase over 2 miles on the same Cheltenham ***card*.' There should be no assumption from this example that the Jenny Mould is a harder challenge than the Bonusprint, though. It is perhaps less common these days to hear about a celebrated punter having a *tilt* at the ***ring***, but racing correspondents will occasionally go quixotic: 'Octogenarian Oliver Carter has developed a reputa-tion for *tilting at windmills*'; 'Goncalo Torrealba and his ilk are big cheeses in their own backyard, yet that serves only as a spur to *tilt* at bigger *windmills* in Dubai.'

Tissue: This emits the on-course layers' forecast of how the betting should open: 'The bookies' *tissue* suggested Top Cees would *trade* around the 5/1 mark, but some have opened him up at 8s and they're hardly getting *knocked over in the rush*.' The term seems to derive from the flimsiness of the paper which punters or bookies used to write on, and it remains apt, since the *tissue* can often be a very superficial guide to the *SPs*. *Tissues* were also required whenever Josh Gifford or Jenny Pitman had a winner.

Toe: 'Silver Patriarch was *done* for *toe* at a crucial part of the race'; 'Their horse simply had too much *toe* for my fellow.' In these examples, *toe* translates as speed, or – perhaps more exactly – *turn of foot*. The only other times you are likely to hear about a horse's *toe* is if it's a question of whether the ground is soft enough for him to *get his toe in*, or if he is *on his toes* in the **preliminaries**. *Toey* is the Australian way of describing a **fizzy** horse but they also have a colloquial expression for a *hard-held* victory: 'Despite *tippy-toeing* over the final stages, the eight-year-old had eleven lengths on his nearest rival.'

Tongue-tied: A runner that has been *tongue-tied* can still be a **talking horse**.

Tool: Rarely pejorative in racing; instead, a ready alternative to **machine**, and usually supported by an adjectival intensifier, as in: 'Watson Lake is going to be *some tool* over fences.' It follows that horses who *tool along* are **travelling** well. The noun provides an alternative to *medium* in tipping columns: 'Place Above looks the *perfect tool* for a back-lay wager.'

Top: 'She likes it *on top*.' This will not be a reference to a female jockey's private life but to a mare's proclivity for firm going. *Of the ground* is often left understood here, as *in the ground* is when a pundit advises that an animal prefers *cut*. Hence the formula *top of the ground*, which can be hyphenated and adjectival: 'Another Rum is a real *top-of-the-ground type*.' *Top* is also popular down under as a contraction of 'top of his form': '"Undoubtedly's nowhere near his *top* and has a lot of *improvement* left in him," said Morphettville trainer Mark Kavanagh.'

Touch: 'It was a good old-fashioned *touch* by Sir Mark, and betting-shop punters *joined in* when they saw the odds *tumbling*.' An alternative to *coup*, with the same sense of *getting on* at a big price before connections' confidence becomes common knowledge. *Touch* was late-Victorian slang for an act of petty theft, but there are usually no pejorative connotations in modern times, since most of us like to see the bookies *run for cover*. Those trying to *land a touch* certainly do not want to see their horse *touched off* in the finish.

Tough: *Toughness* is a quality prized above virtually any other, except in the very top echelons, where a horse has to have *class*. Even there, it is important: as well as suggesting that a horse relishes a battle in a race, it also implies that he stays clear of injury and *stands* his racing well. The regulation simile is *tough as teak*, perhaps also inspired by the colour.

Tractable: 'Lamp's Return has the size for chasing, which just might make her more *tractable*'; 'Arkle, the most intelligent and *biddable* of steeplechasers, submitted to the treatment with equanimity.' Racing vocabulary is drawn to some recondite adjectives, which make more palatable the basic premise that horses are supposed to do what they are told.

Traffic: Only ever mentioned in racing when it means or leads to *traffic trouble*: 'The unlucky second got stuck in *traffic* two furlongs out'; 'Plausabelle's style of racing means that she will encounter *traffic problems* from time to time, but it also makes it hard for the handicapper to get to grips with.' With really *bad traffic*, especially early in a race when runners get *bumped*, you occasionally hear a reference to the fairground: 'Momtic was the main sufferer in that bout of *dodgem cars.' Trouble in running* always seems to mean congestion of this kind rather than a problem with the tack or a horse *breaking down*: 'Alexander Goldrun won the Guineas *trial* by a short head from Misty Heights, overcoming *trouble in running* to lead close home.'

Train on: The classic expression for a *classic horse*: in other words, a colt or filly who has developed physically (and mentally) from the age of two to three and is likely to maintain or improve upon his or her juvenile form: 'On the evidence of Sunday's gallop, Damson has *trained on* and she goes straight to Newmarket.' It can also be used of older horses: 'It's not every four-year-old filly who *trains on*, but Kinnaird is so *straightforward* I've no doubts she can *stand* another season.' A phrase so old that Lord Byron, whose brother-in-law was the Prince Regent's racing manager, used it figuratively about his own ability to continue writing. Horses can also be said to *train off*, but this is much less common (the expression rather than the incidence).

Trappy: Applicable to fences and courses that may prove difficult to negotiate but more likely to refer to the dilemma facing the punter. Tends to be used not of major handicaps with a maximum field – the bookmakers' sales pitch for these is *ultra-competitive* – but of those tricky maidens or novice chases where you could *make a case* for several of the runners: 'The third on the *card* at Salisbury is a *trappy little affair.'*

Travel: A key word, with *on the bridle* usually understood. If you say of a horse, 'He really *travels* in his
races,' the implication is that he has some *class* and
that you mean he *travels well*. But the word is likely to
recur in virtually every account of an actual race,
whatever the outcome: 'He was always *travelling well*
and it took just **hands and heels** to settle the **argument**'; 'He was **never** *travelling* at any stage in the
race and perhaps something was **amiss**.' Occasionally,
journalists will connect the way a horse was **weak**
in the ring with its tame performance: 'Dabaweyaa
travelled as badly in the race as she did in the market.'
The same idea can also turn on the word *move*, as
in this further example: 'Almaydan's pre-race *moves*
were about as exciting as it got with the post-race
comments of *"never better* than **mid-div**" pretty well
summing things up.'

Treatment: Euphemism for very strong *handling*:
'Blowing Wind got the full McCoy *treatment*.' A word
which can combine some sympathy for the horse
being *encouraged* with admiration for the strength of
the jockey's *urgings*.

Trial: This word can be used of a **serious** piece of
home work, or – especially in the United States and
Australia – of a practice *spin* on the racecourse: a
barrier trial is one in which the horse is loaded into
starting stalls for experience. In the British Isles it is
more common to find it referring to races that are a
stepping stone to a bigger prize. Indeed, the titles of
some races, such as the Lingfield Derby *Trial*, or the
Champion Hurdle *Trial* at Haydock, explicitly recognise that they serve this function. Because they tend
to attract **small but select fields**, *trials* are often run
at a *false pace* and the form does not usually *work out*
on the big day itself.

Trip: A ubiquitous term because so much of the skill in training horses lies in finding their optimum race distance. Horses who do *stay* are said to *get* or *see out* the *trip*. Some animals are transformed when they **step up** in *trip* or when they are *dropped* or *come back* in *trip*. Whereas certain unfortunate horses do not seem to have such a thing as an *optimum trip*: 'Master Papa is beginning to *look tripless* as he struggles for pace over two miles but does not seem to *see out* twenty furlongs.' On the flat, *trip* can occasionally turn out to be synonymous with **passage**: 'The runner-up suffered a *trip* of monumentally bad proportions.'

Trotting: This type of racing is popular in continental Europe, especially France, where the simulcast from Vincennes can sometimes prove of more interest to local punters than the Group 1 event going on behind them unobserved. Most *trotting* races involve horse-drawn chariots (*attelés*) but the version where the horses, trying to run as fast as possible in a slow gait, are backed (*montés*) by jockeys riding longer than **John Wayne**'s grandmother, is particularly counter-intuitive. *Trotting* is also the fare of choice in some parts of North America (where it is called *harness racing*) but never in Britain and Ireland (where it is called *rollocks*).

True: The adjective, like its opposite, is most likely to refer to the *pace*: a *truly run* race is conducted at a proper gallop whereas a *falsely run* race probably sees them *walking out* of the stalls. You can also talk about *true* **tests** of stamina or *false patches* of ground.

Try: In racing, you can be criticised for *trying* too little or *trying* too much. *Non-trier* is the classic term for a horse who is not being allowed to **run on its merits**; indeed, the Jockey Club Rule on such conduct is known colloquially as the *non-trier's rule*. Perhaps this is why some trainers are so keen to tell the press that their charge will be *trying for his life* while nevertheless confiding in connections that he will not be *trying too hard*. Eschewing any suggestion that it is shrewd to run horses in an attempt to get their handicap mark down, Mark Johnston has adopted the motto *Always Trying* for his Middleham stable. On the other hand, when a horse is described as *highly tried*, there is a pejorative implication that the trainer is running him at too high a level by pitching the horse into level-weights races or top-class handicaps with little realistic chance. *Over-faced* is another way of putting this but an *overreach* is a technical term for a horse *striking into* himself.

Tune: 'Richard Johnson doesn't merely *get a tune* out of Monkerhostin but the descant as well.' This is the most orchestrated version we have seen of a relatively common trope based on the idea that when a jockey **gets on well** with a particular horse he can also expect to *get a tune* out of him. For trainers, *tuning up* a horse for a big race is a more patient and, if most of them are to be believed, technical matter: see **concert pitch**.

Turn on the taps: Not, as you might expect, a reference to the precautionary actions of the clerk of the course in a dry spell, but to what jockeys – or even the horses themselves – do when they dramatically increase the tempo of the gallop: 'Basically Best Mate and Seebald had *turned on the taps* and were sprinting for home.' We have heard a similar metaphor used in live commentary: 'Wee Robbie begins to really *pour it on*.'

Turn out: Used with two entirely different meanings. Horses are *turned out* for races by their trainers and at the same time they are eligible to win the *Best Turned Out* awards for the efforts of their lad or lass (usually, like Manager of the Month awards in football, a kiss of death). But when animals are **roughed off** for the season they are also *turned out*, this time *into a field*.

Twig: The twigs, usually **birch**, only ever win the attention of commentators in the negative when praise for an impeccable round of jumping is called for: '**Spring-heeled** Pearlyman didn't *touch a twig*.'

Two ways of running: The classic expression for an inconsistent horse, often a bit of a **thinker**, who only puts his *best foot forward* on his **going days**: 'Omni Cosmo Touch, even if he *consents* to start, has *two ways of running*, so it is hard to back him with any confidence here.' See **in and out** for another way of putting it, without necessarily implying that the horse has not been trying his best.

U

Under: 'Tipping Tim is improving *under* Tom Jenks.' Often just a narrative filler in order to name the rider but, as well as conveying the physical position of the horse and jockey, the preposition also intimates the degree of control the latter will have exerted. Conversely, a jockey may allude to the *horsepower* he has at his disposal by using the preposition's slightly more imposing cousin: 'I still had a lot of horse *underneath* me at that point and knew I would **pick** them **up**.'

Under starter's orders: Or simply *under orders* (the *starter's* is often left understood), the official expression for the moment when the runners arc all *installed* or *called in*, ready for the *off*. In betting shops it tells punters that they have seconds left to *get on* (usually the seconds when the person in front of you in the queue is trying to place a **Yankee** on the *virtual* racing simultaneously with an exotic bet on the next at Walthamstow, while collecting his winnings on a race at Turfontein run two weeks ago Wednesday). Earlier warning is given if commentators say, 'They won't be *long* now,' or, 'The *goggles* are *coming down*,' when there are only a few more runners to load or line up (the French word for these moments *at the post* is *imminent*). At racecourses themselves, 'They're *under starter's orders*' is sometimes boomed out over the tannoy by a disembodied yet strident voice. The phrase is pronounced with the same spavined intonation of those taped announcements common at railway stations since privatisation.

Uneasy: When a runner is described as *uneasy*, it does not necessarily mean that the horse himself is anxious, or *awash* with sweat, but that his price is *drifting*, a fact of which the horse itself is **blissfully unaware**: 'Despite being *uneasy* in the market, Tahtheeb did it *nicely* enough.'

Unseated rider: The official term for an incident where a **blunder** by a horse causes the jockey to come off. Rather like wicket-keepers who have conceded byes to balls they think should have been wides, jockeys are very quick to contest the judge's verdict, and it is in these circumstances standard practice to turn the participle into a noun: 'That should never have gone down as *an "unseated"* as the horse was on all fours.'

Unship: 'And Black Humour has *unshipped* his rider at that one.' Marginally more obliging to the jockey than *unseat*, though the usual need for economy (the participle has one less syllable) may be disguised as magnanimity here.

Up: The labels that accompany paintings of *horse and jockey* always draw on the same set prepositional phrase: 'Gimcrack *with* John Pratt *up*'. The *up* may seem a little redundant here (as though you might otherwise wonder which is which), but it remains a beautifully neat way in modern parlance of saying that a jockey has been booked: 'The mare must have every chance with A. P. McCoy *up*.' Such was Fred Archer's popularity in Victorian times that *Archer's up* became a form of morning greeting. This has long since been out of use, though a more recent headline – *Archer's sent down* – did recall it momentarily.

Up and down on the spot: Dressage shows that it is not a physical impossibility for horses to run *up and down on the spot*, but in racing this expression denotes the *shortening stride* of an animal who has become very tired, usually over extreme distances in energy-sapping ground: 'The *toiling* Truckers Tavern is just *running up and down on the spot* back in third.' *Treading water* is another way of putting it, particularly if the going is soft.

Upsides: Never 'alongside' in racing: 'A good shot there of the two leaders *upsides*.'

V

Valet: Jockeys pronounce this word to rhyme with 'pallet'. Any piece of journalism on the day-to-day routine in the **weighing room** shows how crucial *valets* are, although their duties do not seem to extend to jockeys' cars, which are notoriously untidy. John Buckingham is as famous for having been a well-respected *valet* as for winning on 100/1 shot Foinavon after the pile-up in the 1967 National.

Value: Perhaps at the same time as the distinction between 'growth' and 'value' investing in financial markets was in vogue, *value betting* became a fashionable concept in the 1980s, popularised by the *Racing Post's Pricewise* column. Even the *nom de plume* sounds rather like a chain of cash-and-carries, although a list of the main contributors over the years (Coton, Collier and Segal) does have more the air of a firm of lawyers. *Value* bets advised in the column will be guaranteed to *steam in* once *traders* are awake and the *offices* are open. Meanwhile, horses can also be *full value* or *more* than *face value* for a victory: 'Attraction won the Coronation Stakes by two and a half lengths (*value* four) from Majestic Desert.' The little parenthesis here probably *franks the form* even more affirmatively than the observation '*pair clear*'.

Vices: Very specific denomination for three pieces of behaviour often observed in horses confined to stables: *crib-biting*, *weaving* and *windsucking*. The first *vice* is fairly self-explanatory; the second involves the horse bobbing his head convulsively in and out of the stable door; the third is the equine equivalent of smoking whereby the animal bites on the fittings of his box and inhales for all he is worth. It is understood that these *vices* should be disclosed to potential buyers if they have ever been observed. Therefore sales catalogues will, for the most neurotic animals, contain a sentence admitting: 'Has *been seen* to crib-bite, weave and windsuck.' Although horses may have many other vicious character traits *at **home*** – like trying to ***monster*** anybody that comes near them – or on course – like ***hanging*** or otherwise

losing you large amounts of money – these would
never be described as *vices*.

Virtual: The adverb in the set phrase 'made *virtually
all*' serves race-readers admirably when they cannot
quite remember whether the winner did actually
make *every yard* of the running. Betting shops now
screen *virtual racing* every day from places like
Portman Park (which does not need to be an *all-
weather* track because fortunately all weather there is
good) accompanied by the seductive slogan 'There is
nothing *virtual* about a winner.' These words may or
may not be designed to placate old-fashioned cur-
mudgeons like us who still want the horses and the
jockeys and the ground and everything else to be
real. With the new *improved graphics*, the latest
advertising promises that 'you will not believe your
eyes'. Indeed.

Visit: 'Chorist will be *visiting* King's Best.' Such a
visit will not be for the purposes of a singing lesson.

W

Waited with: The preposition may seem to dangle
awkwardly ('Waited with what?'), but a perfectly
standard way of saying that a horse was *dropped out*
or held up: 'As usual Montjeu was *waited with* for the
first mile.'

Walk: If their price is lengthening, horses are said to
take a walk in the market. The metaphor is apposite
since these *drifters* in the betting may take a similarly
leisurely approach to the race. If nobody wants to go on
at the start of a contest and the pace is therefore *fune-*

real, the commentator may say that he or his *granny* could *walk faster*. If he notes later that a horse has *stopped to a walk*, his tone is likely to be less facetious because this usually means that something is *amiss*.

Walk home: 'It's lucky the fences aren't any *stiffer*, otherwise Luke Harvey would be *walking home.'* A nicely ironic idiom, even if *unseated* jockeys are known to cadge a lift back in one of the *ambulances*. Irony would be out of place though when a jockey is said to have *walked away* from a fall (just as a fortunate racing driver might *walk away* from a crash). Occasionally, indeed, there can be a sombre atmosphere surrounding the *walk back* to the *weighing room*, as in the poignant photograph of Mark Pitman making the *long walk back up* the Cheltenham hill towards the packed stands after a fatal fall to his mother's Alekhine in the 1989 Supreme Novices.

Warm order: 'Cool Panic is a *warm order* for this one.' A cliché applied to a horse who is *well backed* before the off, without being quite a *hot* enough *tip* to become the proverbial *steamer*.

Warn off: 'Bradley was initially *warned off* for eight years.' The regulatory term for the ultimate sanction taken against someone who infringes the rules of racing is more graphic and severe-sounding than a mere 'ban'. If it calls to mind the action of a hostile gamekeeper surrounded by baying dogs, it is no coincidence. As owners of Newmarket Heath, the Jockey Club could ban a person from its property and it is this sanction that was extended to prohibiting a miscreant from conducting any activity on a racecourse.

Washing: Horses who are *tailed off* find themselves *out with the washing*. The image can be coloured by commentators for greater effect: 'Forget the rest:

they're *strung out* like Wednesday's *washing.* Unless midweek laundry loads were traditionally much lighter, or Wednesday was the day you did pants, it seems the alliteration must account for this particular choice.

Watched: Preceded by *best*, this makes for a short and sweeter way of saying that a horse has very little chance: 'Moonshot showed some fair form *on the level* earlier in the year but is *best watched* today on his chasing *bow.*' Particularly common in the clipped, but uncontroversial, form summaries found in official racecards. Sometimes in these circumstances connections will not want to watch. More positively, punters can be exhorted to keep an eye on the ring to gauge the chances of very *unexposed* horses: 'She is well bred even if *reportedly backward*, and any *market move* should be *closely watched.*'

Weak: Trainers are surprisingly candid when talking about two-year-olds or young *stores* who have not yet *filled out* their frames: 'He's a big *weak* individual and will be much better next year.' On course, if a horse *weakens* in the market it is usually – but by no means always – the presage to his soon *weakening* in the race: '*weakened* 2f out' is the classic race-reader's shorthand for the point in a contest where a horse has no effective chance.

Weighing room: The *weighing room* is not actually where jockeys must weigh *out* and *in*: this takes place in an anteroom known as *the scales*. But it is appropriate that the dressing room where jockeys and their *valets* are based is named in this way, given that so many riders are faced with a constant *battle* to keep to their *riding weight*. It has also become the metonymic way of referring to the community of jockeys: 'The whole *weighing room* is up in arms about

this ban on mobile phones.' Nobody else is allowed
into this inner sanctum apart from racecourse officials
(and the BBC on Grand National day), which stops
interlopers offering riders bribes or trying to interfere with their tack. It also adds to the glamour and
mystique of the place, which we are told is full of
camaraderie and superstitious ritual. For example,
when a senior jockey retires, the other riders really do
move their kit *up a peg*.

Well in: *Well in*, that phrase heard in nightclubs
up and down the country (and spun out in rare
Hertfordshire vernacular as 'He's *Garden City* with
her'), has a tamer sense in racing: 'The Villager previously turned in a sound effort against *well in* Classic
Native on soft ground at Bangor.' *At the weights* is
understood – the horse being *well in* not so much
with the connections as with our old friend the
handicapper.

Wet sail: What a horse *comes with* when making sudden late progress from the *next* **parish**, the *clouds* or
some other *impossible position*: 'Lammtarra finished
with a *wet sail* on the stands side and just *got up*.' A
metaphor borrowed from yachting, and indeed many
such fast finishers have found their *second wind*.

Whispers: *Whispers* now tend to be trumpeted in
five-inch-high flashing magenta letters in advertisements on Ceefax, or relayed in eight-minute tele-
phone messages at a premium rate, but the idea
remains that if you have reliable inside *information*
on a horse you will want to keep it as quiet as possible so as not to contract the odds *available*. Because
you only hear about *whispers* that have moved the
price, the usage can become fairly contradictory:
'There were *whispers* about this one all week, so that
he started as low as 2/1 *in **places**.' Connections can

also tell everybody in their loudest voice – usually after a win – that their runner was *quietly fancied*. This is probably as close as professional racing gets to *hoarse whispering*.

White face: Seemingly always *big*, the lay equivalent of a *blaze*. Mentioned as a distinguishing trait by grateful commentators when there is no **sheepskin noseband** in sight.

Wind: There was a time when man knew nothing upon the earth faster than a horse. The horse was therefore a paragon of speed (a character in a Voltaire story rushes off 'as fast as a horse at Newmarket') and the only thing comparable to the horse was *the wind*. The mechanical age has certainly taken over (see **aeroplane**, **express train**, **Ferrari**), even though those who **ride out** on the gallops still know how to keep their feet on the ground: 'The best horses are not usually the ones who work like *flying machines* at home.' A horse can sometimes find a *second wind* in a race, but, when mentioned nowadays, *wind* is more likely to be a sign of *problems*, after a jockey or lad has heard *gurgling*, *roaring* or *whistling* noises. Perhaps we should add that such problems are of a respiratory rather than an alimentary nature.

Wings: It is fairly obvious why the white pickets at either side of a fence (now made of plastic for safety reasons) are called *wings*. And even if the hurdles have been removed for a **bumper**, you will still hear references to running *between the wings*. This does not mean that somebody has drifted out of position in a game of rugby. More importantly, the *wings* have become the unit of measure for a jump where a horse has really *stood off*: 'He **pinged** that one from *outside the wings*.' This is the opposite of *getting into* the **roots**. Metaphorical examples can be graphic – 'Ruby says he wishes he'd *winged* him into the second last because the horse loves *going long*' – or even poetic: 'It will be great to see the three of them *winging their way* up that hill at Cheltenham.'

Winner all right: The Irish version of *weighed in*, confirming that the clerk of the scales has checked that each jockey is carrying the same amount after the race as before. Perhaps more punter-friendly, as most bets on a race will be *on the nose*. Whenever somebody *weighs in* light (or if a jockey battling against the scales *weighs in* heavy), connections always plead complete ignorance of the reasons.

Winningmost: 'A. P. McCoy, *winningmost* jump jockey of all time': perhaps it is our imagination, but we see this superlative formulation more in racing than elsewhere, and the effect can be little short of parodic: 'As at 2 January, the 20-year-old *apprentice* from Belfast is the year's *winningmost* jockey.' There is an American variant: 'Russel Baze replaces the late Bill Shoemaker as the second-*winningest* jockey in racing history.'

Winter: National Hunt racing has always been the *winter game* in Britain and Ireland (in no other country does it have the stage completely to itself on *turf*), but the international nature of flat racing now seems largely responsible for having turned the chilly noun into a warm verb, as often as not with Dubai the destination: 'Jonny Ebeneezer *wintered* well over there in the Emirates and looks on *good terms* with **himself**.' The verb can even be transitive: 'We're going to *winter* him in Dubai this year.'

Wobbler: Not a description of a racegoer as he or she exits the bars after the **lucky last**, but of a young thoroughbred who has a neurological disease that

makes him unco-ordinated and very often unwanted:
'Shamardal was almost **put down** as a yearling
because he was a *"wobbler"*.'

Work: The dominant idea in racing is **home** *work*.
When stable lads take out each **lot** in the morning
they are said to be *riding work* which, depending on a
horse's level of fitness, can be *light, easy, strong, fast*
or even *maintenance*: 'Not A Single Doubt did sufficient to *top* him off. He was out there today only to
do *maintenance work*.' The barometer of a horse's
well-being is often an individual *piece of work*: 'He did
two **serious** *pieces of work* this week and I couldn't
be happier with him.' Early in a campaign, trainers
may leave a little **condition** on a horse so that they
have something *left to work on*. But at more important
phases in a season, if a horse *misses work* or is *held up*
in his *work* by a **setback** or the weather, the interrup-
tion can be critical. For references to *work* at the racecourse, see **best work** and **keep up**.

Worry out: 'Blushing Bull was *worried out of it* in the
closing stages.' You could be forgiven for thinking that
the real translation of this sentiment, so often heard
from trainers who have just been *touched off*, is:
'Blushing Bull would have won if that other horse
hadn't gone a bit faster at the end.' But sometimes
there are genuine grounds for believing that the horse
in question likes things *his own way* or **stops** when he
hits the front, and is therefore vulnerable to a *renewed
challenge* from behind. Horses can also *worry* or *spook*
themselves jumping very big fences, hearing very loud
noises, or when racegoers ignore announcements
prohibiting the use of *flash photography*.

Wound up: 'Kitty O'Shea hasn't been *wound up* yet
and can only improve.' When Aidan O'Brien does
wind up Kitty O'Shea *fully* for her target, he will not

be wanting to leave anything *on her*, and she most definitely will not be *needing the race*. The trainer is cast as gunsmith rather than horologist in this further example, which also winds up on the alliteration: 'Knockelly Castle is as *cocked* and ready as a *cowboy's gun*.' A jockey can also be said to be *winding it up* if he gradually increases the pace of a contest when riding from the front. However, horses can get too *wound up* in the **preliminaries**, increasing the chances that they will not *settle* in the race itself.

Wrong: Almost a technical adjective in racing circles to mean 'unwell' or 'injured': 'All my horses were *wrong* at the time so I wouldn't read too much into that run'; 'I'm afraid he's *gone wrong* on his front legs.' The first usage is slightly more common than the second. The close cousin is *amiss*. If a horse is out of the handicap it is said to be *wrong at the weights*: 'Golden Alpha has a lot to do being twelve pounds *wrong*.'

X

X-rated: 'I thought he was dead at Lingfield. It was a real *X-rated* fall.' Certification of this kind is only applied to falls where the jockey is **buried** or the horse does not immediately get up on his *feet all right*.

Y

Yankee: Perhaps the most famous *permutation* bet, which survived competition from the *ITV Seven* and still appears on betting slips, especially on Saturdays, despite the current popularity of the *Scoop6*. A *Yankee* is eleven bets on four horses made up of six doubles, four trebles and an *accumulator* on all four horses. Professional punters believe these multiple bets are for *mugs*, but if are you are betting in very small stakes they are understandably hard to resist.

Yard: Whereas you think about *every inch* for a horse who needs a *trip*, and in terms of *miles* when you have been *beat* out of sight, the *yard* is the correct imperial unit of measure if you are talking about *trailblazers* or *rogues*: 'Pat Fahy's 105-rated hurdler was still *holding the call* after setting out to make *every yard* up front when falling at the final *flight*'; 'We fancied him today but I'm afraid he spat the dummy out and didn't *go* a *yard*.'

Yardstick: When we see a reference to 'that good *yardstick* Celibate', it does not mean that Celibate stands on his own at the side of the course at a certain distance, but that he is a reliable horse who *reproduces* the same standard of *running* each time, and so allows proper study of *collateral form*.

Z

Zest: 'Governor Daniel has been racing with *plenty of zest* of late for one of advancing years.' This is an entirely admirable quality given that so many racehorses can become *stale* through too many races, or *sour* through too many hard ones. *Zest* is preferred to *sparkle* when praising a horse's enthusiasm for the *game*, perhaps to avoid any suggestion that he is too *fizzy*.

Zing: Not as extravagant as *ballooning* but more on a par with *pinging* and *winging*: 'For the first six fences in the Hennessy, Pizarro *zinged*. Then he *guessed*.'